Edward Arber, Philip Sidney

An Apologie for Poetrie

1595

Edward Arber, Philip Sidney

An Apologie for Poetrie
1595

ISBN/EAN: 9783337777678

Printed in Europe, USA, Canada, Australia, Japan

Cover: Foto ©Thomas Meinert / pixelio.de

More available books at **www.hansebooks.com**

English Reprints.

Sir PHILIP SIDNEY.

APOLOGIE FOR POETRIE.

1595.

Edited by EDWARD ARBER, F.S.A.

*Fellow of King's College, London; Hon. Member of the Virginia and Wisconsin Historical Societies;
Examiner in English Language, Literature and History in the University of London;
Professor of English Language and Literature,
Sir Joshia Mason's College, Birmingham.*

BIRMINGHAM

34 WHEELEYS ROAD.

1 April, 1868.

No. 4.

CONTENTS.

CHRONICLE

of

fome of the principal events

in the

LIFE, WORKS, and TIMES

of

Master, afterwards Sir PHILIP SIDNEY,

Courtier, Ambassador, Poet, Romancist, Critic, and Soldier.

---

* Probable or approximate dates.

1553. July 6. Mary succeeds to the crown.

1554. July 25.   Queen Mary marries Philip, King of Spain.
Nov. 29.   PHILIP SIDNEY 'was son of Sir Hen. Sidney by the lady Mary his wife, eldest daughter of Joh. Dudley duke of Northumberland, was born, as 'tis supposed, at Penshurst in Kent, 29 Nov. 1554, and had his Christian name given to him by his father, from K. Philip, then lately married to Queen Mary.'—*Wood, Ath. Oxon.* i. 517. *Ed.* 1813. Philip is the eldest of three sons, and four daughters.

1558. Nov. 17. Elizabeth begins to reign.

1560.   Sir Henry Sidney is made Lord President of Wales, which office he holds till his death. He resides, when in the Principality, chiefly at Ludlow. He is three times Lord Deputy of Ireland, between 1565-67, 1568-71 and 1577-78. He is installed K. G. May 14. 1564.

At Shrewsbury School.

1564. Oct. 17.   Philip Sidney and Fulke Greville, both of the same age,
æt. 9. and who became friends for life, enter Shrewsbury School on the same day.—'*Anno Domini* 1564. 16 *Cal. Nov.*
Philippus Sidney filius et hæres Henrici Sidney Militis de Pensarst in Comit. Cantiæ, et Domini Praesidis confinium Cambriae, nec non Ordinis Garterii Militis.
Foulkus Greyvell filius et hæres Foulki Greyvell Armigeri de Beauchamp Courte in Comit. Warwici. eodem die. School Register: see *Sidneiana* Roxburghe Clube 1837. Fulke Greville thus testifies of his schoolfellow "of whose Youth I will report no other wonder, but thus: That though I lived with him, and knew him from a child, yet I never knew him other than a man: with such staiednesse of mind, lovely, and familiar gravity, as carried grace, and reverence above greater years. His talk ever of knowledge, and his very play tending to enrich his mind: So as even his teachers found something in him to observe, and learn, above that which they had usually read, or taught. Which eminence, by nature, and industry, made his worthy Father stile Sir *Philip* in my hearing (though I unseen) *Lumen familiæ suæ.*" F. Greville, in his posthumous *Life of Sir P. Sidney, p.* 7. *Ed.* 1652.

At Oxford.

1568* Midsummer. "While he was very young, he was sent to Christ
æt. 13 Ch. to be improved in all sorts of learning, and was contemporary there with Rich Carew author of *The Survey of Cornwall*, where continuing till he was about 17 years of age, under the tuition of Dr. Tho. Thornton, canon of that house."—*Wood, idem.*

Travelling Abroad.

1572.	May 25.
	æt. 17.

1572. May 25. The Queen grants Philip Sidney, license to go abroad
æt. 17. with three servants and four horses: (May 26) Leaves London, in the train of the Earl of Lincoln, Ambassador to the French King: (Aug. 9) Charles ix. makes him one of the gentlemen of his Chamber: (Aug. 24) The Massacre of St. Bartholomew. Sidney being in the house of the English Ambassador, Sir Francis Walsingham, is safe: He however soon leaves Paris, journeys by Heidelberg to Frankfort, where he meets Hubert Languet, æt. 54. He stays at Frankfort about nine

1573. Summer. months. They two then go to Vienna : where, after some trips to Hungary, Sidney leaves Languet, and spends eight months in Italy ; chiefly in Venice, Padua, and

1574. Genoa. He returns to Vienna in Nov. Spends his
1575. May 31. winter there (see p. 19), and coming home through the Low Countries; reaches England (May 31. 1575).

1575. æt. 20. Introduced to Court, by his uncle, the E. of Leicester. See p. 6.

July 9–27. Is at the famous reception given by his uncle to the Queen, at Kenilworth. The Court moves to Chartley castle, where Philip is supposed first to have seen *Stella* (Penelope, æt. 13, daughter of Lord Essex, and afterwards Lady Rich). The sonnets *Astrophel and Stella* go on for the next five or six years.

Ambassador.

1577. æt. 22. Sidney is sent as Ambassador, with messages of condo-
Feb. *22. lence to Rodolph II. the new Emperor of Germany, at
June 8. Prague ; and to the two sons of the Frederic III. late Elector Palatine : viz. Lewis (now Elector) and John Casimir. at Heidelberg.

1578. May. On the Court coming to his uncle's, at Wanstead, Sidney writes a masque *The Lady of the May.*
Sidney becomes acquainted with Gabriel Harvey, and through him with Edmund Spenser.

1579. August. Stephen Gosson publishes the *The Schoole of Abuse.*
Oct. 16. E. Spenser writes to G. Harvey, Sidney's idea of it.
Dec. [*Ent. Stat. Hall* 5 Dec.] Spenser's *Shepherds Calendar.*
1580. Sidney writes to the Queen, against her marrying the Duke of Anjou.
Jointly with his sister Mary, translates *Psalms of David.* Writes *The Arcadia.*

Chiefly at Court.

1580. Oct. 18. Sidney writing from Leicester House, to his brother
æt. 25. Robert, æt. 17. (afterwards Earl of Leicester) then travelling in Germany ; gives him, in a long and brotherly letter, his ideas on the study of history. This confidential letter shows that Sidney's mind was, at this time, much occupied with the consideration of subjects dealt with in the *Apologie*, to which it may be considered as a forerunner.
"For the Method of writing Historie, *Boden* hath written at large, yow may reade him, and gather out of many Wordes some Matter. This I thinke in Haste, a Story is either to be considered as a Storie, or as a Treatise, which, besides that, addeth many Thinges for Profite and Ornament ; as a Story, he is nothing but a Narration of Thinges done, with the Beginings, Cawses, and Appendences thereof. . . . . In that Kinde yow haue principally to note the Examples of Vertue or Vice, with their good or evell Successes, the Establishments or Ruines of great Estates, with the Cawses, the Tyme, and Circumstances of the Lawes then write of, the Entrings and Endings of Warrs, and therein, the Stratagems against the Enimy, and the Discipline vpon the Soldiour ; and thus much as a very Historiographer.

Besides this, the Historian makes himselfe a Discourser for Profite, and an Orator, yea a Poet sometimes for Ornament. An Orator, in making excellent Orations, *e re nata*, which are to be marked, but marked with the Note of Rhetoricall Remembrances: A Poet in painting forth the Effects, the Motions, the Whisperings of the People, which though in Disputation, one might say were true, yet who will make them well, shall finde them taste of a Poetical Vaine, and in that Kinde are gallantly to be marked, for though perchance they were not so, yet it is enough they might be so. The last Poynt which tendes to teach Profite, is of a Discourser, which Name I giue to who soeuer speakes, *Non simpliciter de facto, sed de qualitatibus et circumstantijs factj*; and that is it which makes me, and many others, rather note much with our Penn then with our Minde. . . . . This write I to yow in greate Hast, of Method without Method, but with more Leysure and Studie (if I doe not finde some Booke that satisfies) I will venter to write more largely vnto yow." . . . . *Arthur Collin's Letters and Memorials of State*, i. 283-5. *Ed.* 1746.

Chiefly at Court.

1581. Jan. 16–Mar. 18. Parliament sits. Sidney is for the first time a Member.
    Sept. 30. Languet dies at Antwerp.
        Sidney writes *An Apologie for Poetrie*.
1583. Jan. 8. The Queen knights him.
 * Mar. æt. 29. He maries Frances, daughter of Sir F. Walsingham.
1584. Nov. 23.–1585. Mar. 29. Parliament sits. Sidney a second time a member.
        Writes *Discourse in Defence of the Earl of Leicester.*
        His daughter Elizabeth born [afterward the Countess of Rutland].
        Projects an expedition to America, with Sir F. Drake.

Governor of Flushing.

    Nov. 7. Is appointed Governor of Flushing: Nov. 16. Leaves England for the last time: Nov. 21. Assumes his office.
1586. May 5. His father Sir H. Sidney dies at Worcester.
   July 6. Sidney, with 3000 men, surprises Axel.
   Aug. 9. His mother Lady Mary Sidney dies.
   Sept. 22. At the fight at Zutphen, Sidney 'receyved a sore Wounde upon his Thighe, three Fingers above his Knee, the Bone broken quite in Peeces. . . . He was carried afterwards in my barge to *Arnheim.'* E. of Leicester. *See Collin's Memoirs of the Sidneys, p.* 105.
   Oct. 17. Sidney lingers 26 days. His wife and brother join
 2 p.m. æt. 31. him. His last words were—*Love my Memorie, cherish my Friends, their Faith to me may assure you they were honest. But above all, govern your Will and Affections, by the Will and Word of your Creator; in me, beholding the end of this World, with all her Vanities.*

His body was removed (Oct. 24) to Flushing; embarked (Nov. 1) there for conveyance to London; landed (Nov. 5) at Tower-hill, and taken to a house in the Minories, without Aldgate: where it remained, until the public funeral (Feb. 16. 1587) at St. Paul's. England goes into mourning for him.

In place of fuller details of Sidney's life, which will be found in he works of A. Collins, Dr. T. Zouch, and H. R. F. Bourne, we may obtain a better impression of his character, by adducing the independent testimony of four contemporaries, all competent to know the truth, and none apparently exaggerating it.

The first three come to us through Fulke Greville. See *Life*, pp. 31-34.

1. William of Nassau, 'William the Silent,' Prince of Orange, requested Greville to tell his Queen "that if he could judge, her Majesty had one of the ripest, and greatest Counsellours of Estate in Sir *Philip Sidney*, that at this day lived in *Europe*: to the triall of which hee [the Prince] was pleased to leave his owne credit engaged, untill her Majesty might please to employ this Gentleman, either amongst her friends or aenemies."

2. Robert Dudley, Earl of Leicester, his uncle, "told me (after Sir *Philips*, and not long before his own death) that when he undertook the government of the Low Countries, he carryed his Nephew over with him, as one amongst the rest, not only despising his youth for a Counsellor, but withall bearing a hand over him as a forward young man. Notwithstanding in short time he saw this Sun so risen above his Horizen, that both he and all his Stars were glad to fetch light from him. And in the end acknowledged that he held up the honor of his casual authority by him, whilst he lived, and found reason to withdraw himself from that burthen, after his death."

3. Sir Francis Walsingham, his Father-in-law "that wise and active Secretarie . . . . . often confessed to my self, that his *Philip* did so far overshoot him in his own Bow, as those friends which at first were Sir *Philip*'s for this Secretaries sake, within a while became so fully owned, and possest by Sir *Philip*, as now he held them at the second hand, by his Son-in-laws native courtesie."

4. Sir Robert Naunton [b. 1563,—d. Mar. 27, 1635], Master of the Court of Wards, in his posthumous work, entitled *Fragmenta Regalia, or Observations on the late Queen Elizabeth, her times and favourites* [First edition 1641, corrupt. Second edition 1642], gives us the following clear though brief account of Sidney. It is the best contemporary sketch of him that has come down to us.

"He was sonne to Sir *Henry Sydney*. Lord Deputy of *Ireland*, and President of *VVales*, a person of great parts, and in no mean grace with the Queen: his mother was sister to my Lord of *Leicester*, from whence we may conjecture, how the Father stood up in the place of honour, and employment, so that his descent was apparently noble on both sides: For his education, it was such as travell, and the University could afford. or his Tutors infuse, for after an incredible proficiency in all the species of Learning, he left the Academicall life for that of the Court, whither he came by his Vncles invitation, famed afore-hand by a noble report of his accomplishments, which together with the state of his person, framed by a naturall propension to Arms, he soon attracted the good opinion of all men, and was so highly prized in the good opinion of the Queen, that she thought the Court deficient without him: And whereas (through the fame of his deserts) he was in the election for the Kingdome of *Pole*, she refused to further his advancement, not out of emulation, but out of fear to lose the jewell of her times: He married the daughter and sole heir of Sir *Francis Walsingham*, then Secretary of State, a Lady destinated to the Bed of honour, who (after his deplorable death at *Zutphen* in the Netherlands, where he vvas Governour of *Flushing*, at the time of his Vncles being there) vvas married to my Lord of *Essex*, and since his death, to my Lord of Saint *Albons*, all persons of the svvord, and other vvise of great honour and vertue.

They have a very quaint and factious figment of him, That *Mars* and *Mercury* fell at variance vvhose servant he should be; And there is an *Epigrammist* that saith, That Art and Nature had spent their excellencies in his fashioning, and fearing that they should not end what they begun, they bestowed him on Fortune, and Nature stood musing, and amazed to behold her own work. But these are the petulancies of Poets.

Certain it is, He was a noble and matchlesse Gentleman, and it may be justly said without hyperbolyes of fiction, as it was of *Cato Vticensis*, that he seemed to be born to that onely which he went about. *Versatilis ingenii*, as *Plutarch* hath it, but to speak more of him, were to make him lesse." pp. 18—19. Ed. 1642.

At p. 17. of the same work, he gives us an insight of Elizabeth's ideas on Sidney's death.

"I can here adde a true, and no impertinent Story, and that of the last *Mountioy*, who having twice or thrice stol[e]n away into *Brittain*[y] (where under Sir *Iohn Norris* he had then a Company) without the Queen's leave and privity; she sent a Messenger unto him, with a strict charge to the Generall to see him sent home: when he came into the Queens presence, she fell into a kinde of reviling, demanding how he durst go over without her leave; Serve me so (quoth she) once more, and I will lay you fast enough for running; You will never leave it untill you are knockt on the head, as that inconsiderate fellow *Sidney* was: You shall go when I send you, in the mean time see that you lodge in the Court (which was then at *VVhite-Hall*) where you may follow your Book, read and discourse of the Wars."

Án APOLOGIE For POETRIE.

INTRODUCTION.

THE reference, at page 62, to Spenfer's *Shepherd's Calendar* as printed; proves inconteftably, that Sidney wrote his *Apologie* fubfequent to the 5th December, 1579, the date of the licenfing upon entry at Stationer's Hall, of Spenfer's work; the firft edition of which bears the date of 1579, the fecond 1581, and the third 1586?

The earlieft date affignable to the prefent reprint is therefore 1580. Some time fhould, however, be allowed for the *Shepherd's Calendar* to attain to its acknowledged reputation. The date ufually given for the compofition of the *Apologie for Poetrie*, viz., 1581, may therefore be taken as approximately correct.

For the motive to its production is known. It is a carefully prepared anfwer to portions of two works dedicated to Sidney, by another poet, Stephen Goffon; who had but recently forfaken the Stage for the Pulpit. Thefe works were *The Schoole of Abufe*, which appeared about Auguft 1579, and *An Apologie of the Schoole of Abufe*, which was publifhed in the following November.

Edmund Spenfer, writing from Leicefter Houfe, on the 16th October of the fame year, to his friend Gabriel Harvey at Cambridge, incidentally gives us Sidney's opinion of Goffon's firft work.

" Newe Bookes I heare of none, but only of one, that writing a certaine Booke, called *The Schoole of Abufe*, and dedicating it to Maifter *Sidney*, was for hys labor fcorned : if at leafte it be in the goodneffe of that nature to fcorne. Suche follie is it, not to regarde aforehande the inclination and qualitie of him, to whom we dedicate oure Bookes."*

The lateſt date that can poſſibly be aſſigned to this work, is 16th November, 1585, when Sir P. Sidney left England for the laſt time. The probability however is, that the vindication followed ſoon upon the attack.

It were an eaſy taſk, to trace in detail the line of aſſault and defence; but for this we have here no ſpace. Both works being now within eaſy reach of all, ſuch a compariſon may be made by any. It will be better to riſe from the temporal controverſy to the general principles difcuſſed in the preſent work : merely noting that the ultimate point at iſſue between Sidney and Goſſon, ſeems to have been, whether uncleannefs, falſity, and effeminacy were ſeparable or infeparable from poetry.

The *Apologie* is four times the length of thoſe portions of Goſſon's tracts which dealt with the abufes of Poetry. For Sidney took advantage of the occaſion, ' with quiet judgment looking a little deeper into it,' to eſtabliſh, to his own fatisfaction at leaſt, the reafons for the exiſtence at all of Poetry, and the demonſtrations of its ſuperlative excellence. Some of theſe apply lefs forcibly now than in his own time, through the general ſpread of the power of reading among the people; but there is much expoſition of that which will remain for all time.

A book of criticifm on poetry is itſelf but a textbook of further endlefs critical difcuſſion. Anything like a conſideration here of the ſubject-matter of the *Apologie* is not poſſible to us: but it may be well to notice Sidney's uſe of the word Poet and its modern acceptation.

---

* *Three proper and wittie, familiar Letters;* by IMMERITO [Spenſer] and G. H. p. 54. London [Eut. Stat. Hall, 30 June] 1580.

Sidney would have called Bunyan's *Pilgrim's Progress*, Fénelon's *Telemachus*, and Defoe's *Robinson Crusoe*, poems. He defignates Xenophon's *Cyropædia* 'an abfolute Heroic poem.'* Accepting the word Poet in its original and univerfal fenfe of maker; he fays 'There haue beene many moft excellent Poets, that neuer verfified.'* 'One may bee a Poet without verfing, and a verfifier without Poetry;'† 'Verfe being but an ornament and no caufe to Poetry:'* and gives this criterion, 'It is that fayning notable images of vertues, vices, or what els, with that delightfull teaching which muft be the right defcribing note to know a Poet by.'‡ So that in the *Apologie*, Sidney is really defending the whole art and craft of Feigning.

The fcience of definitions progreffed after Sidney's death; and the Idea of Poet became limited to that of Imaginator in verfe. Ben Jonfon, in a pofthumous work—printed fixty years later than the compofition of the *Apologie*—entitled *Timber: or Difcoveries; Made vpon Men and Matter: as they have flow'd out of his daily Readings; or had their refluxe to his peculiar Notion of the Times*, propofes and anfwers three queftions: and in fo doing, eftablifhes and expreffes ‡he modern limitation of the Idea.

What is a Poet?

"*A Poet* is that, which by the Greeks is call'd κατ' ἐξοχὴν, ὁ Ποιητὴς, a Maker, or a fainer: His Art, an Art of imitation, or faining; expreffing the life of man in fit meafure, numbers, and harmony, according to *Ariftotie*: From the word ποιεῖν, which fignifies to make or fayne. Hence, hee is call'd a *Poet*, not hee which writeth in meafure only; but that fayneth and formeth a fable, and writes things like the Truth. For, the Fable and Fiction is (as it were) the forme and Soule of any Poeticall worke, or *Poeme*.

* p. 28.　† p. 49.　‡ p. 29.

What meane you by a Poeme?

A Poeme is not alone any worke, or compofition of
the Poets in many or few verfes; but even one alone
verfe fometimes makes a perfect *Poeme.* As, when
Aeneas hangs up, and confecrates the Armes of *Abas,*
with this Infcription ;
  Aeneas hæc de Danais victoribus arma. And calls
it a *Poeme* or *Carmen.* Such are thofe in *Martiall.*
  Omnia, Caftor, emis : fic fiet, ut omnia vendas.
And *Pauper videri Cinna vult, et eft pauper.*†
So were Horace his *Odes* call'd, *Carmina* ; his
Lirick, Songs. And *Lucretius* defignes a whole booke,
in his fixt :
  Quod in primo quæque carmine claret.
And anciently, all the Oracles were call'd, *Carmina* ;
or, what ever Sentence was exprefs'd, were it much, or
little, it was call'd, an *Epick, Dramatick, Lirike,
Elegiake,* or *Epigrammatike Poeme.*

But, how differs a Poeme from what wee call Poesy?

A Poeme, as I have told you is the worke of the
Poet; the end, and fruit of his labour, and ftudye.
Poefy is his fkill, or Crafte of making ; the very Fiction
it felfe, the reafon, or forme of the worke. And thefe
three voices differ, as the thing done, the doing, and
the doer ; the thing fain'd, the faining, and the fainer :
fo the *Poeme,* the *Poesy,* and the *Poet."*‡
It is to be defired that that word Feigner were re-
leafed from its prefent degradation; and that ennobled,
it might become the modern equivalent to Sidney's
ufe of the word Poet :—a generic term embracing
Poets, Allegorifts, Fabulifts, Romancifts, Novelifts ;
all who "imitate to teach and delight, and to imitate,
borrow nothing of what is, hath been, or fhall be : but
range onely rayned with learned difcretion, into the
diuine confideration of what may be, and fhould be."§

---

* Virgilius Aeneid, lib. 3.   ‡ Workes, ii. 125, 126. Ed. 1641.
† Lib. 8, Epig. 19.   § p. 28.

Sidney's want of appreciation either of the difficulty or excellence of great Profe—for he feems to have thought 'the weighing of each word in just proportion, according to the dignity of the fubject' peculiar to verse; and the diffatisfaction of himfelf and Goffon in Englifh poetry; muft be confidered in connection with the dates of their refpective compofitions. They were both ftanding on the very threfhold of our modern national literature. The men were then alive, who fhould, within a generation—within the fpan of Goffon's life, for Sidney was prematurely cut off—do more to fix our language and to immortalize our literature, than had been or has fince been done. The golden age of Englifh fong was juft beginning. Shakefpeare and Spenfer, the founders of two diftinct fchools of poetry; Ben Jonfon, Fairefax, and a hoft of minor dramatifts, fonneteers, tranflators, and the like; endowed England with noble Verfe. Hooker, Knolles, Bacon, Raleigh, the Tranflators of the authorized Englifh verfion of the Scriptures, and many others of leffer degree, gave us a not lefs worthy Profe. The intellectual life of that generation is a prodigy in our hiftory. What other Chriftian country has produced three contemporaries, such as Shakefpeare, Spenfer, and Bacon? It was an age not only of difcovery all the world round; but of high attainment to new truths both in fact and opinion: not only of the eftablifhment of new proceffes of arriving at Truth; but alfo of the invention of new forms for its expreffion. All that is romantic, chivalrous, frefh, clufters and concentrates round the laft of the Tudors. With the incoming of the Stuarts, with the paffing away of that generation, Englifh Hiftory begins to become flat and ftale, foon to pafs into the ftorm of the Civil Wars, in the midft of which, this outburft of the true old chivalry finally dies out.

But from Goffon and Sidney all this was hidden. They could only look back over the drearinefs of Englifh poetry to Chaucer and Gower: and there was nothing to fhow, that the future might not be even as the paft.

Accepting their works as the current criticifm of the day; we may obtain a meafure of the originality of thefe after-writers. In nothing is this more confpicuous, than in the doctrine of the Unities of action, time and place, in dramatic compofition; fet forth by Ariftotle, and reafferted moft ftrongly, at page 63 of the prefent work. This doctrine the fubfequent Englifh dramatifts refufed to obey as a compulfory law; for recognifing unity of action as the moft obligatory, they neglected or ufed the other two, at their will and pleafure.

One parting teftimony. The *Apologie* bears abundant evidence to the ethereal refinement of Sidney's nature, and to his ecftatic delight in Poefy; in the epithets and epithetic phrafes he gives 'to the peerleffe Poet.' He but defcribes himfelf, in defcribing David, as 'a passionate louer, of that vnfpeakable and euerlafting beautie to be feene by the eyes of the minde, onely cleered by fayth.'* Adopting his own definition of Poefy, may we not, in fome degree at leaft, apply to him, his own defcription of ' our Poet the Monarch.'

" He dooth not only fhow the way, but giueth fo fweete a profpect into the way, as will intice any man to enter into it. Nay, he dooth as if your iourney fhould lye through a fayre Vineyard, at the firft giue you a clufter of Grapes : that full of that tafte, you may long to paffe further. He beginneth not with obfcure definitions, which muft blur the margent with interpretations, and load the memory with doubtfulneffe : but hee commeth to you with words fent in delightfull proportion, either accompanied with, or prepared for the well inchaunting skill of Muficke; and with a tale forfooth he commeth vnto you : with a tale which holdeth children from play, and old men from the chimney corner. And pretending no more, doth intende the winning of the mind from wickedneffe to vertue."†

* p. 24.   † p. 40.

BIBLIOGRAPHY.

AN APOLOGIE FOR POETRIE.

* Editions not feen.

(a) **Issues in the Author's life time.**

None

(b) **Issues since the Author's death.**

I. *As a feparate publication.*

1. 1595. London.   *Editio princeps :* fee title on page 15.
    1 vol. 4to.
20. 1752. Glafgow.   ' The Defence of Poefy ' by Sir Philip
    1 vol. 8vo.   Sidney, Knt.
22. 1810. London.   ' The Defence of Poefy,' the author
    1 vol. 4to.   Sir Philip Sidney, Knight. [Ed. by
     Lord THURLOW, ' who, after giving a
     few copies to his friends, fuppreffed the
     remainder' *M. S. note in copy in Britifh
     Mufeum* 70. *f.* 22.]
25. 1 April 1868.   *Englifh Reprints :* fee title at page 1.
   London. 1 vol. 8vo.

II. *With other works.*

2. 1598. London.   The Covnteffe of Pembrokes Arcadia.
    1 vol. fol.   Written by Sir Philip Sidney Knight.
     Now the *third* time publifhed, with
     fundry new additions of the fame Au-
     thor. Imprinted for William Pon-
     fonbie. ' The Defence of Poefie ' oc-
     cupies pp 491—518.
3. * 1599. Edinburgh.   The fame title as No. 2. Now the
    1 vol. fol.   *third* time publifhed. &c. Publifhed by.
     Robert. Walde-graue. *Lownd. p.* 2395.
4. 1605. London.   The fame title as No. 2. Now the
    1 vol. fol.   *fovrth* time pvblifhed &c. Imprinted
     for MATTHEVV. LOVVNES. ' The De-
     fence of Poefy ' occupies pp 491—518.
5. 1613. London.   The fame title as No. 2. Now the
    1 vol. fol.   *fovrth* time publifhed &c. Imprinted
     for *H. L.* for *Simon Waterfon.* ' The
     Defence of Poefie' occupies pp 491-518.
6. 1621. Dublin.   The fame title as No. 2 Now the
    1 vol. fol.   *fift* time publifhed &c. Printed by the
     Societie of STATIONERS. ' The De-
     fence of Poefie ' occupies pp 503—530.
7. *1623 London.   The fame title as No. 2. Now the
   [1621?] 1 vol. fol   *fifth* time publifhed. *Lowndes.*
8. *1622. London.   The fame title as No. 2. Now the *fixt*
    1 vol. fol.   time publifhed Imprinted by H. L.
     for S. Waterfon. *Lowndes.*

9. * 1627. London.   The fame title as No. 2. Now the
     1 vol. fol   *fixt* time publifhed. Imprinted by W.
             S. for S. Waterfon *Lowndes.*

10. * 1629. London.   The fame title as No. 2. Now the
     1 vol. fol. *feventh* time publifhed. Printed for H.
             L. and R. V. *Lowndes.*

11. 1633. London.   The fame title as No. 2. Now the
     1 vol. fol. *eighth* time publifhed. Printed for
             SIMON WATERSON and R. YOUNG.
             'The Defence of Poefie' occupies pp
             540—566.

12. * 1638. London.   The fame title as No. 2. Now the
     1 vol. fol. *ninth* time publifhed *Lowndes.*

13. * 1655. London.   The fame title as No. 2. *Tenth edition*
     1 vol.   Printed for DU GARD. *Lowndes.*

14. * 1662. London.   The fame title as No. 2. *Eleventh*
     1 vol. fol. *edition. Lowndes.*

15. * 1674. London.   The fame title as No. 2. *Twelfth*
     1 vol. fol. *edition.* LOWNDES.

16. 1674. London.   The Countefs of Pembroke's Arcadia
     1 vol. fol. written by Sir Philip Sidney, Knight.
             The Thirteenth Edition With his Life
             and Death; a brief Table of the prin-
             cipal Heads, and fome other new Addi-
             tions. Printed for George Calvert.
             'The Defence of Poefie' occupies pp.
             540—566.

17. * 1683. ——
     —— fol. Watts quotes an edition of the Ar-
             cadia, &c., of this year. *Lowndes.*

18. 1724-5. London.   The works of the Honourable Sir
     3 vols. 8vo. Philip Sidney; Kt. *The Fourteenth*
             Edition. 'The Defense of Poefy' occu-
             pies iii. 1—52 : the pagination recom-
             mencing, in the middle of this volume,
             with it.

19. * 1739. Dublin.   The Works, in Profe and Verfe.
     3 vols. 12mo. *Lowndes.*

21. 1787. London.   Sir Philip Sydney's 'Defence of
     1 vol. 8vo. Poetry': and 'Obfervations on Poetry
             and Eloquence' from the 'Difcoveries'
             of Ben Jonfon [Ed. by Dr JOSEPH
             WARTON.]

23. 1829. Oxford.   The mifcellaneous works of Sir
     1 vol. 8vo. Philip Sidney, Knt. Ed. by WILLIAM
             GRAYS of Magdalen College, and the
             Inner Temple.   'The Defence of
             Poefy' occupies pp 1—66.

24. * 1860. Boston, U.S.   A reprint of No. 23. *Lowndes.*
     1 vol. 8vo.

AN

APOLOGIE

for Poetrie.

Written by the right noble, vertuous, *and learned Sir* Phillip
Sidney, *Knight.*

Odi profanum vulgus, et arceo

AT LONDON,

Printed for *Henry Olney*, and are to be fold at
his fhop in Paules Church-yard, at the figne
of the George, neere to Cheap-gate.
Anno. 1595.

To the Reader.

THE ſtormie Winter (deere Chyldren of the Muſes, which hath ſo long held backe the glorious Sun-ſhine of diuine Poeſie, is heere by the ſacred pen-breathing words of diuine Sir *Philip Sidney*, not onely chaſed from our fame-inuiting Clyme, but vtterly for euer baniſht eternitie : then gracciouſly regreet the perpetuall ſpring of euer-growing inuention, and like kinde Babes, either enabled by wit or power, help to ſupport me poore Midwife, whoſe daring aduenture, hath deliuered from Obliuions wombe, this euer-to-be-admired wits miracle. Thoſe great ones, who in them-ſelues haue interr'd this bleſſed innocent, wil with *Aeſculapius* condemne me as a detractor from their Deities: thoſe who Prophet-like haue but heard preſage of his coming, wil (if they wil doe wel) not onely defend, but praiſe mee, as the firſt publique bewrayer of Poeſies *Meſsias*. Thoſe who neither haue ſeene, thereby to interre, nor heard, by which they might be inflamed with deſire to ſee, let them (of duty) plead to be my Champions, ſith both theyr ſight and hearing, by mine incurring blame is ſeaſoned. Excellent Poeſie, (ſo created by this Apologie,) be thou my Defendreſſe ; and if any wound mee, let thy beautie (my ſoules Adamant) recure mee : if anie commend mine endeuored hardiment, to them commend thy moſt diuineſt fury as a winged incouragement ; ſo ſhalt thou haue deuoted to thee, and to them obliged

Henry Olney.

Foure Sonnets written by *Henrie Conſtable*
to Sir *Phillip Sidneys* ſoule.

Glue pardon (bleſſed Soule) to my bold cryes
If they (importund) interrupt thy ſong,
   Which nowe with ioyfull notes thou ſing'ſt, among
   The Angel-Quiriſters of heau'nly ſkyes:
Giue pardon eake (ſweet Soule) to my ſlow cries,
   That ſince I ſaw thee now it is ſo long,
   And yet the teares that vnto thee belong,
   To thee as yet they did not ſacrifice:
I did not know that thou wert dead before,
   I did not feele the griefe I did ſuſteine,
   " The greater ſtroke aſtoniſheth the more,
   " Aſtoniſhment takes from vs ſence of paine,
I ſtood amaz'd when others teares begun,
And now begin to weepe, when they haue doone.

SWeet Soule which now with heau'nly ſongs dooſt tel
Thy deare Redeemers glory, and his prayſe,
   No meruaile though thy ſkilful Muſe, aſſayes
   The ſongs of other ſoules there to excell:
For thou didſt learne to ſing diuinely well,
   Long time before thy fayre, and glittering rayes
   Encreas'd the light of heau'n, for euen thy layes
   Moſt heauenly were, when thou on earth didſt dwel:
When thou didſt on the earth ſing Poet-wiſe,
   Angels in heau'n pray'd for thy company,
   And now thou ſing'ſt with Angels in the ſkies,
   Shall not all Poets praiſe thy memory?
And to thy name ſhall not their works giue fame
When as their works be ſweetned by thy name?

EVen as when great mens heires cannot agree :
So eu'ry vertue now for part of thee doth fue,
Courage prooues by thy death thy hart to be his due,
Eloquence claimes thy tongue, and fo doth courtefy,
Inuention knowledge fues, Iudgment fues memory,
Each faith thy head is his, and what end fhall enfue
Of this ftrife know I not, but this I know for true,
That whofoeuer gaines the fute, the loffe haue wee
Wee, (I meane all the world) the loffe to all pertaineth,
Yea they which gaine doe loofe, and onely thy
foule gaineth,
For loofing of one life, two liues are gained then :
Honor thy courage mou'd, courage thy death did
giue,
Death, courage, honor, makes thy foule to liue,
Thy foule to liue in heau'n, thy name in tongues of men.

GReat *Alexander* then did well declare
How great was his vnited Kingdomes might,
When eu'ry Captaine of his Army might
After his death with mighty Kings compare :
So now we fee after thy death, how far
Thou doft in worth furpaffe each other Knight,
When we admire him as no mortall wight,
In whom the leaft of all thy vertues are :
One did of *Macedon* the King become,
Another fat in the *Egiptian* throne,
But onely *Alexanders* felfe had all :
So curteous fome, and fome be liberall,
Some witty, wife, valiaunt, and learned fome,
But King of all the vertues thou alone.

Henry Conftable.

An Apologie for Poetrie.

Hen the right vertuous *Edward VVotton*, and I, were at the Emperors Court together, wee gaue our felues to learne horfemanfhip of *Iohn Pietro Pugliano :* one that with great commendation had the place of an Efquire in his ftable. And hee, according to he fertilnes of the Italian wit, did not onely afoord vs the demonftration of his practife, but fought to enrich our mindes with the contemplations therein, which hee thought moft precious. But with none I remember mine eares were at any time more loden, then when (either angred with flowe paiment, or mooued with our learner-like admiration,) he exercifed his fpeech in the prayfe of his facultie. Hee fayd, Souldiours were the nobleft eftate of mankinde, and horfemen, the nobleft of Souldiours. Hee fayde, they were the Maifters of warre, and ornaments of peace : fpeedy goers, and ftrong abiders, triumphers both in Camps and Courts. Nay, to fo vnbeleeued a poynt hee proceeded, as that no earthly thing bred fuch wonder to a Prince, as to be a good horfeman. Skill of gouernment, was but a Pedanteria in comparifon : then would hee adde certaine prayfes, by telling what a peerleffe beaft a horfe was. The onely feruiceable Courtier without flattery, the beaft of moft beutie, faithfulnes, courage, and fuch more, that if I had not beene a peece of a Logician before I came to him, I think he would haue perfwaded mee to haue wifhed my felfe a horfe. But thus much at leaft with his no fewe words hee draue into me, that felfe-loue is better then any guilding to make that feeme gorgious, wherein our felues are parties. VVherein, if *Pugliano* his ftrong

affection and weake arguments will not fatisfie you, I
wil giue you a neerer example of my felfe, who (I
knowe not by what mifchance) in thefe my not old
yeres and ideleft times, hauing flipt into the title of a
Poet, am prouoked to fay fomthing vnto you in the
defence of that my vnelected vocation, which if I
handle with more good will then good reafons, beare
with me, fith the fcholler is to be pardoned that
foloweth the fteppes of his Maifter.   And yet I muft
fay, that as I haue iuft caufe to make a pittiful defence
of poore Poetry, which from almoft the higheft eftimation of learning, is fallen to be the laughingftocke
of children.   So haue I need to bring fome more
auaileable proofes: fith the former is by no man
barred of his deferued credite, the filly latter hath
had euen the names of Philofophers vfed to the
defacing of it, with great danger of ciuill war among
the Mufes.   And firft, truly to al them that profefsing
learning inueigh againft Poetry, may iuftly be ob-
iected, that they goe very neer to vngratfulnes, to
feek to deface that, which in the nobleft nations and
languages that are knowne, hath been the firft light-
giuer to ignorance, and firft Nurfe, whofe milk by
little and little enabled them to feed afterwards of
tougher knowledges: and will they now play the Hedg-
hog, that being receiued into the den, draue out his
hoft? or rather the Vipers, that with theyr birth kill
their Parents?   Let learned Greece in any of her
manifold Sciences, be able to fhew me one booke,
before *Mufæus, Homer*, and *Hefiodus*, all three nothing
els but Poets.   Nay, let any hiftorie be brought, that
can fay any VVriters were there before them, if they
were not men of the fame fkil, as *Orpheus, Linus*,
and fome other are named: who hauing beene the
firft of that Country, that made pens deliuerers of
their knowledge to their pofterity, may iuftly chal-
lenge to bee called their Fathers in learning: for not
only in time they had this priority (although in it felf
antiquity be venerable) but went before them, as

caufes to drawe with their charming fweetnes, the wild
vntamed wits to an admiration of knowledge. So as
Amphion was fayde to moue ftones with his Poetrie,
to build Thebes. And *Orpheus* to be liftened to by
beaftes, indeed, ftony and beaftly people. So among
the Romans were *Liuius, Andronicus,* and *Ennius.* So
in the Italian language, the firft that made it afpire to
be a Treafure-houfe of Science, were the Poets *Dante,
Boccace,* and *Petrarch.* So in our Englifh were *Gower*
and *Chawcer.*

After whom, encouraged and delighted with theyr
excellent fore-going, others haue followed, to beautifie
our mother tongue, as wel in the fame kinde as in
other Arts.   This did fo notably fhewe it felfe, that
the Phylofophers of Greece, durft not a long time
appeare to the worlde but vnder the masks of Poets.
So *Thales, Empedocles,* and *Parmenides,* fange their
naturall Phylofophie in verfes : fo did *Pythagoras* and
Phocilides their morrall counfells : fo did *Tirteus* in war
matters, and *Solon* in matters of policie : or rather,
they beeing Poets, dyd exercife their delightful vaine
in thofe points of higheft knowledge, which before
them lay hid to the world.   For that wife *Solon* was
directly a Poet, it is manifeft, hauing written in verfe,
the notable fable of the Atlantick Iland, which was
continued by *Plato.*

And truely, euen *Plato,* whofoeuer well confider-
eth, fhall find, that in the body of his work, though
the infide and ftrength were Philofophy, the fkinne as
it were and beautie, depended moft of Poetrie : for
all ftandeth vpon Dialogues, wherein he faineth many
honeft Burgeffes of Athens to fpeake of fuch matters,
that if they had been fette on the racke, they would
neuer haue confeffed them.   Befides, his poetical defcribing the circumftances of their meetings, as the
well ordering of a banquet, the delicacie of a walke,
with enterlacing meere tales, as *Giges* Ring, and
others, which who knoweth not to be flowers of Poetrie, did neuer walke into *Appolos* Garden.

. And euen Hiſtoriographers, (although theyr lippes
founde of things doone, and veritie be written in theyr
fore-heads,) haue been glad to borrow both faſhion,
and perchance weight of Poets. So *Herodotus* enti-
tuled his Hiſtorie, by the name of the nine Muſes :
and both he and all the reſt that followed him, either
ſtole or vſurped of Poetrie, their paſſionate deſcribing
of paſsions, the many particularities of battailes, which
no man could affirme : or if that be denied me, long
Orations put in the mouthes of great Kings and Captaines, which it is certaine they neuer pronounced.
So that truely, neyther Phyloſopher nor Hiſtoriogra-
pher, coulde at the firſt haue entred into the gates of
populer iudgements, if they had not taken a great paſ-
port of Poetry, which in all Nations at this day wher
learning floriſheth not, is plaine to be ſeene : in all
which they haue ſome feeling of Poetry. In Turky,
beſides their lawe-giuing Diuines, they haue no other
VVriters but Poets. In our neighbour Countrey Ireland, where truelie learning goeth very bare, yet are
theyr Poets held in a deuoute reuerence. Euen
among the moſt barbarous and ſimple Indians where
no writing is, yet haue they their Poets, who make
and ſing ſongs which they call *Areytos*, both of theyr
Aunceſtors deedes, and praiſes of theyr Gods. A ſuffi-
cient probabilitie, that if euer learning come among
them, it muſt be by hauing theyr hard dull wits ſoft-
ned and ſharpened with the ſweete delights of Poetrie. For vntill they find a pleaſure in the exerciſes
of the minde, great promiſes of much knowledge, will
little perſwade them, that knowe not the fruites of
knowledge. In VVales, the true remnant of the
auncient Brittons, as there are good authorities to
ſhewe the long time they had Poets, which they called
Bardes : ſo thorough all the conqueſts of Romaines,
Saxons, Danes, and Normans, ſome of whom did ſeeke
to ruine all memory of learning from among them, yet
doo their Poets euen to this day, laſt ; ſo as it is not
more notable in ſoone beginning then in long continu-

ing. But since the Authors of most of our Sciences were the Romans, and before them the Greekes, let vs a little stand vppon their authorities, but euen so farre as to see, what names they haue giuen vnto this now scorned skill.

Among the Romans a Poet was called *Vates*, which is as much as a Diuiner, Fore-seer, or Prophet, as by his conioyned wordes *Vaticinium* and *Vaticinari*, is manifest : so heauenly a title did that excellent people bestow vpon this hart-rauishing knowledge. And so farre were they carried into the admiration thereof, that they thought in the chaunceable hitting vppon any such verses, great fore-tokens of their following fortunes were placed. VVhereupon grew the worde of *Sortes Virgilianæ*, when by suddaine opening *Virgils* booke, they lighted vpon any verse of hys making, whereof the histories of the Emperors liues are full : as of *Albinus* the Gouernour of our Iland, who in his childe-hoode mette with this verse

Arma amens capio nec sat rationis in armis.

And in his age performed it, which although it were a very vaine, and godles superstition, as also it was to think that spirits were commaunded by such verses, whereupon this word charmes, deriued of *Carmina* commeth, so yet serueth it to shew the great reuerence those wits were helde in. And altogether not without ground, since both the Oracles of *Delphos* and *Sibillas* prophecies, where wholy deliuered in verses. For that same exquisite obseruing of number and measure in words, and that high flying liberty of conceit proper to the Poet, did seeme to haue some dyuine force in it.

And may not I presume a little further, to shew the reasonablenes of this worde *Vates* ? And say that the holy *Dauids* Psalmes are a diuine Poem ? If I doo, I shall not do it without the testimonie of great learned men, both auncient and moderne : but euen the name Psalmes will speake for mee, which being interpreted, is nothing but fonges Then that it is fully written in meeter, as all learned Hebricians agree, although the rules be not yet fully found. Laftly and principally, his handeling his prophecy, which is meerely poetical. For what els is the awaking his muficall inftruments? The often and free changing of perfons? His notable *Profopopeias*, when he maketh you as it were, fee God comming in his Maieftie. His telling of the Beaftes ioyfulnes, and hills leaping, but a heauenlie poefie: wherein almoft hee fheweth himfelfe a pafsionate louer, of that vnfpeakable and euerlafting beautie to be feene by the eyes of the minde, onely cleered by fayth. But truely nowe hauing named him, I feare mee I feeme to prophane that holy name, applying it to Poetrie, which is among vs throwne downe to fo ridiculous an eftimation: but they that with quiet iudgements will looke a little deeper into it, fhall finde the end and working of it fuch, as beeing rightly ap-plyed, deferueth not to bee fcourged out of the Church of God.

But now, let vs fee how the Greekes named it, and howe they deemed of it. The Greekes called him a Poet, which name, hath as the moft excellent, gone thorough other Languages. It commeth of this word *Poiein*, which is, to make: wherein I know not, whether by lucke or wifedome, wee Englifhmen haue mette with the Greekes, in calling him a maker: which name, how high and incomparable a title it is, I had rather were knowne by marking the fcope of other Sciences, then by my partiall allegation.

There is no Arte deliuered to mankinde, that hath not the workes of Nature for his principall obiect, without which they could not confift, and on which they fo depend, as they become Actors and Players as it were, of what Nature will haue fet foorth. So doth the Aftronomer looke vpon the ftarres, and by that he feeth, fetteth downe what order Nature hath taken therein. So doe the Geometrician, and Arithmetician, in their diuerfe forts of quantities. So doth the

Mufitian in times, tel you which by nature agree,
which not. The naturall Philofopher thereon hath his
name, and the Morrall Philofopher ftandeth vpon the
naturall vertues, vices, and pafsions of man ; and followe Nature (faith hee) therein, and thou fhalt not
erre. The Lawyer fayth what men haue determined.
The Hiftorian what men haue done. The Grammarian
fpeaketh onely of the rules of fpeech, and the Retho-
rician, and Logitian, confidering what in Nature will
foonest proue and perfwade, thereon giue artificial rules,
which ftill are compaffed within the circle of a ques-
tion, according to the propofed matter. The Phifition
waigheth the nature of a mans bodie, and the nature
of things helpeful, or hurtefull vnto it. And the Meta-
phifick, though it be in the feconde and abftract no-
tions, and therefore be counted fupernaturall : yet doth
hee indeede builde vpon the depth of Nature : onely
the Poet, difdayning to be tied to any fuch fubiection,
lifted vp with the vigor of his owne inuention, dooth
growe in effect, another nature, in making things either
better then Nature bringeth forth, or quite a newe
formes fuch as neuer were in Nature, as the *Heroes*,
Demigods, *Cyclops*, *Chimeras*, *Furies*, and fuch like :
fo as hee goeth hand in hand with Nature, not in-
clofed within the narrow warrant of her guifts, but freely
ranging onely within the Zodiack of his owne wit.
  Nature neuer fet forth the earth in fo rich tapiftry,
as diuers Poets haue done, neither with plefant riuers,
fruitful trees, sweet smelling flowers : nor whatsoeuer
els may make the too much loued earth more louely.
Her world is brafen, the Poets only deliuer a golden:
but let thofe things alone and goe to man, for whom
as the other things are, fo it feemeth in him her vttermoft cunning is imployed, and knowe whether fhee
haue brought foorth fo true a louer as *Theagines*, so
conftant a friende as *Pilades*, fo valiant a man as
Orlando, fo right a Prince as *Xenophons Cyrus*: fo
excellent a man euery way, as *Virgils Aeneas* : neither
let this be iestingly conceiued, becaufe the works of

the one be effensiall : the other, in imitation or fiction, for any vnderſtanding knoweth the ſkil of the Artificer: ſtandeth in that *Idea* or fore-conceite of the work, and not in the work it ſelfe. And that the Poet hath that *Idea*, is manifeſt, by deliuering them forth in ſuch excellencie as hee hath imagined them. VVhich de-liuering forth also, is not wholie imaginatiue, as we are wont to ſay by them that build Caſtles in the ayre : but ſo farre ſubſtantially it worketh, not onely to make a *Cyrus*, which had been but a particuler excel-lencie, as Nature might haue done, but to beſtow a *Cyrus* vpon the worlde, to make many *Cyrus's*, if they wil learne aright, why, and how that Maker made him.

Neyther let it be deemed too ſawcie a compariſon to ballance the higheſt poynt of mans wit with the effi-cacie of Nature : but rather giue right honor to the heauenly Maker of that maker : who hauing made man to his owne likenes, ſet him beyond and ouer all the workes of that ſecond nature, which in nothing hee ſheweth ſo much as in Poetrie: when with the force of a diuine breath, he bringeth things forth far ſur-paſſing her dooings, with no ſmall argument to the incredulous of that firſt accurſed fall of *Adam :* ſith our erected wit, maketh vs know what perfection is, and yet our infected will, keepeth vs from reaching vnto it. But theſe arguments wil by fewe be vnder-ſtood, and by fewer granted. Thus much (I hope) will be giuen me, that the Greekes with some probabilitie of reaſon, gaue him the name aboue all names of learn-ing. Now let vs goe to a more ordinary opening of him, that the trueth may be more palpable : and ſo I hope, though we get not ſo vnmatched a praiſe as the Etimologie of his names wil grant, yet his very des-cription, which no man will denie, ſhall not iuſtly be barred from a principall commendation.

Poeſie therefore is an arte of imitation, for ſo *Aris-totle* termeth it in his word *Mimeſis*, that is to ſay, a repreſenting, counterfetting, or figuring foorth : to

fpeake metaphorically, a fpeaking picture : with this
end, to teach and delight ; of this haue beene three
feuerall kindes. The chiefe both in antiquitie and
excellencie, were they that did imitate the inconceiuable
excellencies of GOD. Such were, *Dauid* in his
Pfalmes, *Salomon* in his song of Songs, in his Eccle-
fiaftes, and Prouerbs : *Mofes* and *Debora* in theyr
Hymnes, and the writer of *Iob* ; which befide other,
the learned *Emanuell Tremilius* and *Francifcus Iunius*,
doe entitle the poeticall part of the Scripture. Againft
these none will fpeake that hath the holie Ghoft in due
holy reuerence.

In this kinde, though in a full wrong diuinitie, were
Orpheus, Amphion, Homer in his hymes, and many
other, both Greekes and Romaines : and this Poefie
muft be vfed, by whofoeuer will follow *S. Iames* his
counfell, in finging Pfalmes when they are merry :
and I knowe is vfed with the fruite of comfort by fome,
when in forrowfull pangs of their death-bringing
finnes, they find the confolation of the neuer-leauing
goodneffe.

The fecond kinde, is of them that deale with
matters Philofophicall ; eyther morrall, as *Tirteus,
Phocilides* and *Cato*, or naturall, as *Lucretius* and
Virgils Georgicks : or Aftronomicall, as *Manilius*, and
Pontanus : or hiftorical, as *Lucan* : which who miflike,
the faulte is in their iudgements quite out of tafte,
and not in the fweet foode of fweetly vttered knowledge. But becaufe thys fecond forte is wrapped
within the folde of the propofed fubiect, and takes
not the courfe of his owne inuention, whether they
properly be Poets or no, let Gramarians difpute :
and goe to the thyrd, indeed right Poets, of whom
chiefly this queftion arifeth ; betwixt whom, and thefe
fecond is fuch a kinde of difference, as betwixt the
meaner fort of Painters, (who counterfet onely fuch
faces as are fette before them) and the more excellent : who hauing no law but wit, beftow that in
cullours vpon you which is fitteft for the eye to fee :

as the conſtant, though lamenting looke of *Lucrecia*, when ſhe puniſhed in her ſelfe an others fault.

VVherein he painteth not *Lucrecia* whom he neuer ſàwe, but painteth the outwarde beauty of ſuch à vertue : for theſe third be they which moſt properly do imitate to teach and delight, and to imitate, borrow nothing of what is, hath been, or ſhall be : but range onely rayned with learned diſcretion, into the diuine conſideration of what may be, and ſhould be. Theſe bee they, that as the firſt and moſt noble ſorte, may iuſtly bee termed *Vates*, ſo theſe are waited on in the excellen[te]ſt languages and beſt vnderſtandings, with the fore deſcribed name of Poets : for theſe indeede doo meerely make to imitate : and imitate both to delight and teach : and delight to moue men to take that good-nes in hande, which without delight they would flye as from a ſtranger. And teach, to make them know that goodnes whereunto they are mooued, which being the nobleſt ſcope to which euer any learning was directed, yet want there not idle tongues to barke at them. Theſe be ſubdiuided into ſundry more ſpeciall deno-minations. The moſt notable bee the *Heroick*, *Lirick*, *Tragick*, *Comick*, *Satirick*, *Iambick*, *Elegiack*, *Paſtorall*, and certaine others. Some of theſe being termed according to the matter they deale with, ſome by the ſorts of verſes they liked beſt to write in, for indeede the greateſt part of Poets have apparelled their poeticall inuentions in that numbrous kinde of writing which is called verſe : indeed but apparelled, verſe being but an ornament and no cauſe to Poetry : ſith there haue beene many moſt excellent Poets, that neuer verſified, and now ſwarme many verſifiers that neede neuer aunſwere to the name of Poets. For *Xenophon*, who did imitate ſo excellently, as to giue vs *effigiem iuſti imperij*, the portraiture of a iuſt Empire vnder the name of *Cyrus*, (as *Cicero* ſayth of him) made therein an abſolute heroicall Poem.

So did *Heliodorus* in his ſugred inuention of that picture of loue in *Theagines* and *Cariclea*, and yet

both thefe writ in Profe : which I fpeak to fhew, that
it is not riming and verfing that maketh a Poet, no
more then a long gowne maketh an Aduocate: who
though he pleaded in armor fhould be an Aduocate
and no Souldier. But it is that fayning notable images
of vertues, vices, or what els, with that delightfull
teaching which muft be the right defcribing note to
know a Poet by : although indeed the Senate of Poets
hath chofen verfe as their fitteft rayment, meaning, as
in matter they paffed all in all, fo in maner to goe
beyond them : not fpeaking (table talke fafhion or
like men in a dreame,) words as they chanceably fall
from the mouth, but peyzing each fillable of each
worde by iuft proportion according to the dignitie of
the fubieɗ.

Nowe therefore it fhall not bee amiffe firft to waigh
this latter fort of Poetrie by his works, and then by
his partes; and if in neyther of thefe Anatomies hee be
condemnable, I hope wee fhall obtaine a more fauour-
able fentence. This purifing of wit, this enritching
of memory, enabling of iudgment, and enlarging of
conceyt, which commonly we call learning, vnder
what name foeuer it com forth, or to what immediat
end foeuer it be direɗed, the final end is, to lead
and draw vs to as high a perfeɗion, as our degenerate
foules made worfe by theyr clayey lodgings, can be
capable of. This according to the inclination of the
man, bred many formed imprefsions, for fome that
thought this felicity principally to be gotten by knowledge, and no knowledge to be fo high and heauenly,
as acquaintance with the ftarres, gaue themfelues to
Aftronomie; others, perfwading themfelues to be *Demigods* if they knewe the caufes of things, became naturall
and fupernaturall Philofophers, fome an admirable
delight drew to Muficke : and fome, the certainty of
demonftration, to the Mathematickes. But all, one,
and other, hauing this fcope to knowe, and by knowledge to lift vp the mind from the dungeon of the
body, to the enioying his owne diuine effence. But

when by the ballance of experience it was found, that
the Aſtronomer looking to the ſtarres might fall into a
ditch, that the enquiring Philoſopher might be blinde
in himſelfe, and the Mathematician might draw foorth
a ſtraight line with a crooked hart: then loe, did
proofe the ouer ruler of opinions, make manifeſt, that
all theſe are but ſeruing Sciences, which as they haue
cach a priuate end in themſelues, ſo yet are they all
directed to the higheſt end of the miſtres Knowledge,
by the Greekes called *Arkitecktonike*, which ſtands, (as
I thinke) in the knowledge of a mans ſelfe, in the
Ethicke and politick conſideration, with the end of
well dooing and not of well knowing onely; euen as
the Sadlers next end is to make a good ſaddle : but
his farther end, to ſerue a nobler facultie, which
is horſemanſhip, ſo the horſemans to ſouldiery, and
the Souldier not onely to haue the ſkill, but to performe the practiſe of a Souldier : ſo that the ending
end of all earthly learning, being vertuous action,
thoſe ſkilles that moſt ſerue to bring forth that, haue
a moſt iuſt title to bee Princes ouer all the reſt:
wherein if wee can ſhewe the Poets noblenes, by ſetting him before his other Competitors, among whom
as principall challengers ſtep forth the morrall Philo-
ſophers, whom me thinketh, I ſee comming towards
me with a ſullen grauity, as though they could not
abide vice by day light, rudely clothed for to witnes
outwardly their contempt of outward things, with
bookes in their hands agaynſt glory, whereto they
ſette theyr names, ſophiſtically ſpeaking againſt ſub-
tility, and angry with any man in whom they ſee the
foule fault of anger : theſe men caſting larges as they
goe, of Definitions, Diuiſions, and Diſtinctions, with
a ſcornefull interogatiue, doe ſoberly aske, whether
it bee poſsible to finde any path, ſo ready to leade
a man to vertue, as that which teacheth what vertue
is ? and teacheth it not onely by deliuering forth
his very being, his cauſes, and effects : but alſo, by
making known his enemie vice, which muſt be de-

ſtroyed, and his comberſome ſeruant Paſsion, which
muſt be maiſtered, by ſhewing the generalities that
contayneth it, and the ſpecialities that are deriued from
it. Laſtly, by playne ſetting downe, how it extendeth
it ſelfe out of the limits of a mans own little world,
to the gouernment of families, and maintayning of
publique ſocieties.

The Hiſtorian, ſcarcely giueth leyſure to the Mo-
raliſt, to ſay ſo much, but that he loden with old
Mouſe-eaten records, authoriſing himſelfe (for the
moſt part) vpon other hiſtories, whoſe greateſt
authorities, are built vpon the notable foundation of
Heare-ſay, hauing much a-doe to accord differing
VVriters, and to pick trueth out of partiality, better
acquainted with a thouſande yeeres a goe, then with
the preſent age : and yet better knowing how this
world goeth, then how his owne wit runneth : curious
for antiquities, and inquiſitiue of nouelties, a wonder
to young folkes, and a tyrant in table talke, denieth
in a great chafe, that any man for teaching of vertue, and vertuous actions, is comparable to him.
I am *Lux vitæ, Temporum Magiſtra, Vita memoriæ,
Nuncia vetuſtatis. &c.*

The Phyloſopher (ſayth hee) teacheth a diſputa-
tiue vertue, but I doe an actiue : his vertue is excellent in the dangerleſſe Academie of *Plato*, but mine
ſheweth foorth her honorable face, in the battailes of
Marathon, Pharſalia, Poitiers, and *Agincourt.* Hee
teacheth vertue by certaine abſtract conſiderations,
but I onely bid you follow the footing of them that
haue gone before you. Olde-aged experience, goeth
beyond the fine-witted Phyloſopher, but I giue the
experience of many ages. Laſtly, if he make the
Song-booke, I put the learners hande to the Lute :
and if hee be the guide, I am the light.

Then woulde hee alledge you innumerable examples, conferring ſtorie by ſtorie, how much the
wiſeſt Senatours and Princes, haue beene directed by
the credite of hiſtory, as *Brutus, Alphonſus* of *Aragon*,
and who not, if need bee ? At length, the long lyne

of theyr difputation maketh a poynt in thys, that tne
one giueth the precept, and the other the example.

Nowe, whom fhall wee finde (fith the queftion
ftandeth for the higheft forme in the Schoole of learning) to bee Moderator? Trulie, as me feemeth, the
Poet; and if not a Moderator, euen the man that
ought to carrie the title from them both, and much
more from all other feruing Sciences. Therefore
compare we the Poet with the Hiftorian, and with the
Morrall Phylofopher, and, if hee goe beyond them both,
no other humaine fkill can match him. For as for the
Diuine, with all reuerence it is euer to be excepted,
not only for hauing his fcope as far beyonde any of
thefe, as eternitie exceedeth a moment, but euen for
pafsing each of thefe in themfelues.

And for the Lawyer, though *Ius* bee the Daughter
of Iuftice, and Iuftice the chiefe of Vertues, yet
becaufe hee feeketh to make men good, rather *Formi-
dine pœnæ*, then *Virtutis amore*, or to fay righter, dooth
not indeuour to make men good, but that their euill
hurt not others : hauing no care fo hee be a good Citti-
zen ; how bad a man he be. Therefore, as our wickedneffe maketh him necefsarie, and necefsitie maketh
him honorable, fo is hee not in the deepeft trueth to
ftande in rancke with thefe ; who all indeuour to take
naughtines away, and plant goodneffe euen in the
fecreteft cabinet of our foules. And thefe foure are
all, that any way deale in that confideration of mens
manners, which beeing the fupreme knowledge, they
that beft breed it, deferue the beft commendation.

The Philofopher therfore and the Hiftorian, are
they which would win the gole : the one by precept,
the other by example. But both not hauing both,
doe both halte. For the Philofopher, fetting downe
with thorny argument the bare rule, is fo hard ot
vtterance, and fo miftie to bee conceiued, that one
that hath no other guide but him, fhall wade in him
till hee be olde, before he fhall finde fufficient caufe to
bee honeft : for his knowledge ftandeth fo vpon the
abftract and generall, that happie is that man who

may vnderſtande him, and more happie, that can applye what hee dooth vnderſtand.

On the other ſide, the Hiſtorian wanting the precept, is ſo tyed, not to what ſhoulde bee, but to what is, to the particuler truth of things, and not to the general reaſon of things, that hys example draweth no neceſſary confequence, and therefore a leſſe fruitfull doctrine.

Nowe dooth the peereleſſe Poet performe both: for whatſoeuer the Philoſopher ſayth ſhoulde be doone, hee giueth a perfect picture of it in ſome one, by whom hee preſuppoſeth it was done. So as hee coupleth the generall notion with the particuler example. A perfect picture I ſay, for hee yeeldeth to the powers of the minde, an image of that whereof the Philoſopher beſtoweth but a woordiſh defcription : vvhich dooth neyther ſtrike, pierce, nor poſſeſſe the ſight of the ſoule, ſo much as that other dooth.

For as in outward things, to a man that had neuer ſeene an Elephant or a Rinoceros, who ſhould tell him moſt exquiſitely all theyr ſhapes, cullour, bigneſſe, and perticular markes : or of a gorgeous Pallace, the Architecture, with declaring the full beauties, might well make the hearer able to repeate as it were by rote, all hee had heard, yet ſhould neuer ſatiſfie his inward conceits, with being witnes to it ſelfe of a true liuely knowledge : but the ſame man, as ſoone as hee might ſee thoſe beaſts well painted, or the houſe wel in moddel, ſhould ſtraightwaies grow without need of any defcription, to a iudicial comprehending of them, ſo no doubt the Philoſopher with his learned definition, bee it of vertue, vices, matters of publick policie, or priuat gouernment, repleniſheth the memory with many infallible grounds of wiſdom : which notwithſtanding, lye darke before the imaginatiue and iudging powre, if they bee not illuminated or figured foorth by the ſpeaking picture of Poeſie.

Tullie taketh much paynes and many times not without poeticall helpes, to make vs knowe the force loue of our Countrey hath in vs. Let vs but heare

old *Anchifes* fpeaking in the middeft of Troyes flames,
or fee *Vliffes* in the fulnes of all *Calipfo's* delights,
bewayle his abfence from barraine and beggerly
Ithaca. Anger the *Stoicks* say, was a short maddnes,
let but *Sophocles* bring you *Aiax* on a ftage, killing
and whipping Sheepe and Oxen, thinking them the
Army of Greeks, with theyr Chiefetaines *Agamemnon*
and *Menelaus*, and tell mee if you haue not a more
familiar infight into anger, then finding in the Schoole-
men his *Genus* and difference. See whether wifdome
and temperance in *Vliffes* and *Diomedes*, valure in
Achilles, friendfhip in *Nifus*, and *Eurialus*, euen to
an ignoraunt man, carry not an apparent fhyning :
and contrarily, the remorfe of confcience in *Oedipus*,
the foone repenting pride of *Agamemnon*, the felfe-
deuouring crueltie in his Father *Atreus*, the violence
of ambition in the two *Theban* brothers, the fowre-
fweetnes of reuenge in *Medæa*, and to fall lower, the
Terentian Gnato, and our *Chaucers* Pandar, fo ex-
preft, that we nowe vfe their names to fignifie their
trades. And finally, all vertues, vices, and pafsions,
so in their own naturall feates layd to the viewe, that
wee feeme not to heare of them, but cleerely to fee
through them. But euen in the moft excellent deter-
mination of goodnes, what Philofophers counfell can
fo redily direct a Prince, as the fayned *Cyrus* in
Xenophon? or a vertuous man in all fortunes, as *Aeneas*
in *Virgill*? or a whole Common-wealth, as the way of
Sir *Thomas Moores Eutopia*? I fay the way, becaufe
where Sir *Thomas Moore* erred, it was the fault of the
man and not of the Poet, for that way of patterning a
Common-wealth was moft abfolute, though hee perchaunce hath not fo abfolutely perfourmed it : for the
queftion is, whether the fayned image of Poefie, or
the regular inftruction of Philofophy, hath the more
force in teaching : wherein if the Philofophers haue
more rightly fhewed themfelues Philofophers, then
the Poets haue obtained to the high top of their pro-
feffion, as in truth,

————————*Mediocribus effe poëtis,*
Non Dij, non homines, non conceffere Columnæ:
It is I fay againe, not the fault of the Art, but that
by fewe men that Arte can bee accomplifhed.

Certainly, euen our Sauiour Chrift could as well haue
giuen, the morrall common places of vncharitablenes
and humblenes, as the diuine narration of *Diues* and
Lazarus: or of difobedience and mercy, as that
heauenly difcourfe of the loft Child and the gratious
Father; but that hys through-fearching wifdom,
knewe the eftate of *Diues* burning in hell, and of
Lazarus being in *Abrahams* bofome, would more
conftantly (as it were) inhabit both the memory and
iudgment.   Truly, for my felfe, mee feemes I fee before my eyes the loft Childes difdainefull prodigality,
turned to enuie a Swines dinner : which by the learned
Diuines, are thought not hiftoricall acts, but inftructing
Parables. For conclufion, I fay the Philofopher teacheth,
but he teacheth obfcurely, fo as the learned onely can
vnderftande him: that is to fay, he teacheth them that
are already taught, but the Poet is the foode for the
tendereft ftomacks, the Poet is indeed the right
Popular Philofopher, whereof *Efops* tales giue good
proofe : whofe pretty Allegories, ftealing vnder the
formall tales of Beaftes, make many, more beaftly
then Beafts, begin to heare the found of vertue from
thefe dumbe fpeakers.

But now may it be alledged, that if this imagining
of matters be fo fitte for the imagination, then muft
the Hiftorian needs furpaffe, who bringeth you images
of true matters, fuch as indeede were doone, and not
fuch as fantaftically or falfely may be fuggefted to
haue been doone.   Truely *Ariftotle* himfelfe in his
difcourfe of Poefie, plainely determineth this queftion,
faying, that Poetry is *Philofophoteron* and *Spoudaioteron*,
that is to fay, it is more Philofophicall, and more
ftudioufly ferious, then hiftory.   His reafon is, becaufe
Poefie dealeth with *Katholou*, that is to fay, with the
vniuerfall confideration ; and the hiftory with *Kathe-*

kaſton, the perticuler; nowe ſayth he, the vniuerſall
wayes what is fit to bee ſayd or done, eyther in likelihood or neceſsity, (which the Poeſie conſidereth in his
impoſed names,) and the perticuler, onely mark's,
whether *Alcibiades* did, or ſuffered, this or that. Thus
farre *Ariſtotle*: which reaſon of his, (as all his) is moſt
full of reaſon. For indeed, if the queſtion were whether
it were better to haue a perticular acte truly or falſly
ſet down : there is no doubt which is to be choſen, no
more then whether you had rather haue *Veſpaſians*
picture right as hee was, or at the Painters pleaſure
nothing reſembling. But if the queſtion be for your
owne vſe and learning, whether it be better to haue it
ſet downe as it ſhould be, or as it was : then certainely
is more doctrinable the fained Cirus of *Xenophon* then
the true *Cyrus* in *Iuſtine*: and the fayned *Aeneas* in
Virgil, then the right *Aeneas* in *Dares Phrigius*.

As to a Lady that deſired to faſhion her countenance to the beſt grace, a Painter ſhould more benefite
her to portraite a moſt ſweet face, wryting *Canidia*
vpon it, then to paynt *Canidia* as ſhe was, who *Horace*
ſweareth, was foule and ill fauoured.

If the Poet doe his part a-right, he will ſhew you in
Tantalus, *Atreus*, and ſuch like, nothing that is not to
be ſhunned. In *Cyrus*, *Aeneas*, *Vliſſes*, each thing to
be followed; where the Hiſtorian, bound to tell things
as things were, cannot be liberall (without hee will be
poeticall) of a perfect patterne : but as in *Alexander*
or *Scipio* himſelfe, ſhew dooings, ſome to be liked, ſome
to be miſliked. And then how will you diſcerne what to
followe but by your owne diſcretion, which you had
without reading *Quintus Curtius*? And whereas a
man may ſay, though in vniuerſall conſideration of
doctrine the Poet preuaileth ; yet that the hiſtorie, in
his ſaying ſuch a thing was doone, doth warrant a man
more in that hee ſhall follow.

The aunſwere is manifeſt, that if hee ſtande vpon
that was ; as if hee ſhould argue, becauſe it rayned
yeſterday, therefore it ſhoulde rayne to day, then

indeede it hath fome aduantage to a grofe conceite: but if he know an example onlie, informes a conie&ured likelihood, and fo goe by reafon, the Poet dooth fo farre exceede him, as hee is to frame his example to that which is moft reafonable: be it in warlike, politick, or priuate matters; where the Hiftorian in his bare *VVas*, hath many times that which wee call fortune, to ouer-rule the beft wifedome. Manie times, he muft tell euents, whereof he can yeelde no caufe: or if hee doe, it muft be poeticall; for that a fayned example, hath afmuch force to teach, as a true example: (for as for to mooue, it is cleere, fith the fayned may bee tuned to the higheft key of pafsion) let vs take one example, wherein a Poet and a Hiftorian doe concur.

Herodotus and *Iuftine* do both teftifie, that *Zopirus*, King *Darius* faithful feruaunt, feeing his Maifter long refifted by the rebellious *Babilonians*, fayned himfelfe in extreame difgrace of his King: for verifying of which, he caufed his own nofe and eares to be cut off: and fo flying to the *Babylonians*, was receiued: and for his knowne valour, fo far credited, that hee did finde meanes to deliuer them ouer to *Darius*. Much like matter doth *Liuie* record of *Tarquinius* and his fonne. *Xenophon* excellently faineth fuch another ftratageme, performed by *Abradates* in *Cyrus* behalfe. Now would I fayne know, if occafion bee prefented vnto you, to ferue your Prince by fuch an honeft difsimulation, why you doe not as well learne it of *Xenophons* fiction, as of the others verity: and truely fo much the better, as you fhall faue your nofe by the bargaine: for *Abradates* did not counterfet fo far. So then the beft of the Hiftorian, is fubiect to the Poet; for whatfoeuer action, or faction, whatfoeuer counfell, pollicy, or warre ftratagem, the Hiftorian is bound to recite, that may the Poet (if he lift) with his imitation make his own; beautifying it both for further teaching, and more delighting, as it pleafeth him: hauing all, from *Dante* his heauen, to hys hell, vnder the authoritie of his penne. VVhich if I be asked what Poets haue done fo, as I might well name fome, yet fay I, and fay againe, I fpeak of the Arte, and not of the Artificer.

Nowe, to that which commonly is attributed to the prayfe of hiftories, in refpect of the notable learning is gotten by marking the fucceffe, as though therein a man fhould fee vertue exalt.-d, and vice punifhed. Truely that commendation is peculiar to Poetrie, and farre of from Hiftory. For indeede Poetrie euer fetteth vertue fo out in her beft cullours, making Fortune her wel-wayting hand-mayd, that one muft needs be enamored of her. VVell may you fee *Vliffes* in a ftorme, and in other hard plights ; but they are but exercifes of patience and magnanimitie, to make them fhine the more in the neere-following profperitie. And of the contrarie part, if euill men come to the ftage, they euer goe out (as the Tragedie VVriter anfwered, to one that mifliked the fhew of fuch perfons) fo manacled, as they little animate folkes to followe them. But the Hiftorian, beeing cap-tiued to the trueth of a foolifh world, is many times a terror from well dooing, and an incouragement to vn-brideled wickednes.

For, fee wee not valiant *Milciades* rot in his fetters ? The iuft *Phocion*, and the accomplifhed *Socrates*, put to death like Traytors? The cruell *Seuerus* liue profperoufly? The excellent *Seuerus* miferably mur-thered ? *Sylla* and *Marius* dying in theyr beddes? *Pompey* and *Cicero* flaine then, when they would haue thought exile a happineffe ?

See wee not vertuous *Cato* driuen to kyll himfelfe ? and rebell *Cæfar* fo aduaunced, that his name yet after 1600. yeares, lafteth in the higheft honor ? And marke but euen *Cæfars* own words of the fore-named *Sylla,* (who in that onely did honeftly, to put downe his difhoneft tyrannie,) *Literas nefciuit,* as if want of learning caufed him to doe well. Hee meant it not by Poetrie, which not content with earthly plagues, deuifeth new punifhments in hel for Tyrants : nor yet

by Philofophie, which teacheth *Occidendos effe,* but no
doubt by fkill in Hiftorie : for that indeede can affoord
your *Cipfelus, Periander, Phalaris, Dionifius,* and I
know not how many more of the fame kennell, that
speede well enough in theyr abhominable vniuftice
or vfurpation. I conclude therefore, that hee excel-
leth Hiftorie, not onely in furnifhing the minde with
knowledge, but in fetting it forward, to that which
deferueth to be called and accounted good : which fetting forward, and moouing to well dooing, indeed fetteth the Lawrell crowne vpon the Poet as victorious,
not onely of the Hiftorian, but ouer the Phylofopher :
howfoeuer in teaching it may bee queftionable.

For fuppofe it be granted, (that which I fuppofe
with great reafon may be denied,) that the Philofopher in refpect of his methodical proceeding, doth
teach more perfectly then the Poet : yet do I thinke,
that no man is fo much *Philophilofophos,* as to compare
the Philofopher in moouing, with the Poet.

And that moouing is of a higher degree then
teaching, it may by this appeare : that it is wel nigh
the caufe and the effect of teaching. For who will
be taught, if hee bee not mooued with defire to be
taught ? and what fo much good doth that teaching
bring forth, (I fpeak ftill of morrall doctrine) as that
it moooueth one to doe that which it dooth teach ? for
as *Ariftotle* fayth, it is not *Gnofis,* but *Praxis* muft be
the fruit. And howe *Praxis* cannot be, without being
moooued to practife, it is no hard matter to confider.

The Philofopher fheweth you the way, hee infor-
meth you of the particularities, as well of the tedious-
nes of the way, as of the pleafant lodging you fhall
haue when your iourney is ended, as of the many by-
turnings that may diuert you from your way. But
this is to no man but to him that will read him, and
read him with attentiue ftudious painfulnes. VVhich
conftant defire, whofoeuer hath in him, hath already
paft halfe the hardnes of the way, and therefore is beholding to the Philofopher but for the other halfe.

Nay truely, learned men haue learnedly thought, that where once reafon hath fo much ouer-maftred pafsion, as that the minde hath a free defire to doe well, the inward light each minde hath in it felfe, is as good as a Philofophers booke ; feeing in nature we know it is wel, to doe well, and what is well, and what is euill, although not in the words of Arte, which Philofophers beftowe vpon vs. For out of naturall conceit, the Philofophers drew it, but to be moued to doe that which we know, or to be mooued with defire to knowe, *Hoc opus: Hic labor eft.*

Nowe therein of all Sciences, (I fpeak ftill of humane, and according to the humane conceits) is our Poet the Monarch. For he dooth not only fhow the way, but giueth fo fweete a profpect into the way, as will intice any man to enter into it. Nay, he dooth as if your iourney should lye through a fayre Vineyard, at the firft giue you a clufter of Grapes : that full of that tafte, you may long to paffe further. He beginneth not with obfcure definitions, which muft blur the margent with interpretations, and load the memory with doubtfulneffe : but hee commeth to you with words sent in delightfull proportion, either accompanied with, or prepared for the well inchaunting skill of Muficke ; and with a tale forfooth he commeth vnto you : with a tale which holdeth children from play, and old men from the chimney corner. And pretending no more, doth intende the winning of the mind from wickedneffe to vertue : euen as the childe is often brought to take moft wholfom things, by hiding them in such other as haue a pleafant taft : which if one fhould beginne to tell them, the nature of *Aloes,* or *Rubarb* they fhoulde receiue, woulde fooner take their Phificke at their eares, then at their mouth. So is it in men (moft of which are childifh in the beft things, till they bee cradled in their graues,) glad they will be to heare the tales of *Hercules, Achilles, Cyrus,* and *Aeneas;* and hearing them, muft needs heare the right defcription of wifdom, valure, and iuftice ; which, if they had

been barely, that is to fay, Philofophically fet out,
they would fweare they bee brought to fchoole againe.
That imitation wherof Poetry is, hath the moft con-
ueniency to Nature of all other, in fomuch, that as
Ariftotle fayth, thofe things which in themfelues are
horrible, as cruell battailes, vnnaturall Monfters, are
made in poeticall imitation delightfull. Truely I haue
knowen men, that euen with reading *Amadis de Gaule,*
(which God knoweth wanteth much of a perfect
Poefie) haue found their harts mooued to the exercife
of courtefie, liberalitie, and efpecially courage.

VVho readeth *Aeneas* carrying olde *Anchifes* on his
back, that wifheth not it were his fortune to perfourme
fo excellent an acte? VVhom due not the words of
Turnus mooue? (the tale of *Turnus,* hauing planted his
image in the imagination,)

        ————————*Fugientem hæc terra videbit,*
Vfque adeone mori miferum eft?————————

VVhere the Philofophers, as they fcorne to delight, fo
muft they bee content little to mooue: fauing wrang-
ling, whether Vertue bee the chiefe, or the onely good:
vvhether the contemplatiue, or the actiue life doe excell: which *Plato* and *Boethius* well knew, and therefore made Miftres Philofophy, very often borrow the
mafking rayment of Poefie. For euen thofe harde
harted euill men, who thinke vertue a fchoole name,
and knowe no other good, but *indulgere genio,* and
therefore defpife the auftere admonitions of the Philofopher, and feele not the inward reafon they ftand
vpon; yet will be content to be delighted: which is
al, the good felow Poet feemeth to promife: and fo
fteale to fee the forme of goodnes (which feene they
cannot but loue) ere themfelues be aware, as if they
tooke a medicine of Cherries. Infinite proofes of the
ftrange effects of this poeticall inuention might be
alledged, onely two fhall ferue, which are fo often
remembred, as I thinke all men knowe them.
The one of *Menenius Agrippa,* who when the whole

people of Rome had refolutely deuided themfelues
from the Senate, with apparant fhew of vtter ruine:
though hee were (for that time) an excellent Oratour,
came not among them, vpon truft of figuratiue
fpeeches, or cunning infinuations: and much leffe,
with farre fet *Maximes* of Phylofophie, which (efpecially
if they were *Platonick,*) they muft haue learned
Geometrie before they could well haue conceiued:
but forfooth he behaues himfelfe, like a homely, and
familiar Poet. Hee telleth them a tale, that there
was a time, when all the parts of the body made a
mutinous confpiracie againft the belly, which they
thought deuoured the fruits of each others labour:
they concluded they would let fo vnprofitable a fpen-
der starue. In the end, to be fhort, (for the tale is
notorious, and as notorious that it was a tale,) with
punifhing the belly, they plagued themfelues. This
applied by him, wrought fuch effect in the people, as
I neuer read, that euer words brought forth but then, fo
fuddaine and fo good an alteration; for vpon reafonable conditions, a perfect reconcilement enfued.
The other is of *Nathan* the Prophet, who when the
holie *Dauid* had fo far forfaken God, as to confirme
adulterie with murther: when hee was to doe the tendereft office of a friende, in laying his owne fhame
before his eyes, fent by God to call againe fo chofen a
feruant: how doth he it? but by telling of a man,
whose beloued Lambe was vngratefullie taken from
his bofome: the applycation moft diuinely true, but
the difcourfe it felfe, fayned: which made *Dauid,* (I
fpeake of the fecond and inftrumentall caufe) as in a
glaffe, to fee his own filthines, as that heauenly Pfalme
of mercie wel teftifieth.

By thefe therefore examples and reafons, I think it
may be manifeft, that the Poet with that fame hand of
delight, doth draw the mind more effectually, then any
other Arte dooth, and fo a conclufion not vnfitlie
enfueth: that as vertue is the moft excellent refting
place for all worldlie learning to make his end of: fo

Poetrie, beeing the moſt familiar to teach it, ana moſt
princelie to moue towards it, in the moſt excellent
work, is the moſt excellent workman.   But I am
content, not onely to decipher him by his workes,
(although works in commendation or diſprayſe, muſt
euer holde an high authority,) but more narrowly will
examine his parts: ſo that (as in a man) though altogether may carry a preſence ful of maieſtie and
beautie, perchance in ſome one defectious peece, we
may find a blemiſh: now in his parts, kindes, or
Species, (as you liſt to terme them) it is to be noted,
that ſome Poeſies haue coupled together two or three
kindes, as Tragicall and Comicall, wher-vpon is riſen,
the Tragi-comicall.   Some in the like manner haue
mingled Proſe and Verſe, as *Sanazzar* and *Boetius*.
Some haue mingled matters Heroicall and Paſtorall.
But that commeth all to one in this queſtion, for if
ſeuered they be good, the coniunction cannot be hurtfull.   Therefore perchaunce forgetting ſome, and leauing
ſome as needleſſe to be remembred, it ſhall not be
amiſſe in a worde to cite the ſpeciall kindes, to ſee
what faults may be found in the right vſe of them.

Is it then the Paſtorall Poem which is miſliked?
(for perchance, where the hedge is loweſt, they will
ſooneſt leape ouer.)   Is the poore pype diſdained,
which ſometime out of *Melibeus* mouth, can ſhewe the
miſerie of people, vnder hard Lords, or rauening Souldiours?   And again, by *Titirus*, what bleſſednes is
deriued to them that lye loweſt from the goodneſſe of
them that ſit higheſt? Sometimes, vnder the prettie tales
of VVolues and Sheepe, can include the whole conſiderations of wrong dooing and patience.   Sometimes
ſhew, that contention for trifles, can get but a trifling
victorie.   VVhere perchaunce a man may ſee, that euen
Alexander and *Darius*, when they ſtraue who ſhould
be Cocke of thys worlds dunghill, the benefit they got,
was, that the after-liuers may ſay,

Hæc memini et victum fruſtra contendere Thirſin:
Ex illo Coridon, Coridon eſt tempore nobis.

Or is it the lamenting Elegiack, which in a kinde hart would mooue rather pitty then blame, who bewailes with the great Philoſopher *Heraclitus*, the weakenes of man-kind, and the wretchednes of the world : who ſurely is to be prayſed, either for compaſsionate accompanying iuſt cauſes of lamentation, or for rightly paynting out how weake be the paſsions of wofulneſſe. Is it the bitter, but wholſome Iambick, which rubs the galled minde, in making ſhame the trumpet of villanie, with bolde and open crying out againſt naughtines ; Or the Satirick, who

Omne vaſer vitium, ridenti tangit amico ?

VVho ſportingly neuer leaueth, vntil hee make a man laugh at folly, and at length aſhamed, to laugh at himſelfe : which he cannot auoyd, without auoyding the follie. VVho while

Circum præcordia ludit.

giueth vs to feele, how many head-aches a paſſionate life bringeth vs to. How when all is done,

Eſt vlubris animus ſi nos non deficit æquus ?

No perchance it is the Comick, whom naughtie Play-makers and Stage-keepers, have iuſtly made odious. To the argument of abuſe, I will anſwer after. Onely thus much now is to be ſaid, that the Comedy is an imitation of the common errors of our life, which he repreſenteth, in the moſt ridiculous and ſcornefull ſort that may be. So as it is impoſsible, that any beholder can be content to be ſuch a one.

Now, as in Geometry, the oblique muſt bee knowne as wel as the right : and in Arithmetick, the odde aſwell as the euen, ſo in the actions of our life, who ſeeth not the filthines of euil, wanteth a great foile to perceiue the beauty of vertue. This doth the Comedy handle ſo in our priuate and domeſtical matters, as with hearing it, we get as it were an experience, what is to be looked for of a nigardly *Demea :* of a crafty *Danus :* of a flattering *Gnato :* of a vaine glorious

Thrafo : and not onely to know what effects are to be
expected, but to know who be fuch, by the fignifying
badge giuen them by the Comedian. And little
reafon hath any man to fay, that men learne euill by
feeing it so fet out : fith as I fayd before, there is no man
liuing, but by the force trueth hath in nature, no fooner
feeth thefe men play their parts, but wifheth them in
Piftrinum : although perchance the fack of his owne
faults, lye fo behinde hys back, that he feeth not
himfelfe daunce the fame meafure : whereto, yet nothing can more open his eyes, then to finde his own
actions contemptibly fet forth. So that the right vfe
of Comedy will (I thinke) by no body be blamed, and
much leffe of the high and excellent Tragedy, that
openeth the greateft wounds, and fheweth forth the
Vicers, that are couered with Tiffue : that maketh
Kinges feare to be Tyrants, and Tyrants manifeft their
tirannicall humors : that with fturring the affects of
admiration and commiferation, teacheth, the vncer-
tainety of this world, and vpon how weake foundations
guilden roofes are builded. That maketh vs knowe,

Qui fceptra fæuus, duro imperio regit,
Timet timentes, metus in authorem redit.

But how much it can mooue, *Plutarch* yeeldeth a
notable teftimonie, of the abhominable Tyrant,
Alexander Phercus ; from whofe eyes, a Tragedy wel
made, and reprefented, drewe aboundance of teares :
who without all pitty, had murthered infinite nombers,
and fome of his owne blood. So as he, that was not
afhamed to make matters for Tragedies, yet coulde not
refift the fweet violence of a Tragedie.

And if it wrought no further good in him, it was,
that he in defpight of himfelfe, withdrewe himfelfe
from harkening to that, which might mollifie his
hardened heart. But it is not the Tragedy they doe
miflike : For it were too abfurd to caft out fo excellent a reprefentation of whatfoeuer is moft worthy to
be learned. Is it the Liricke that moft difpleafeth,

who with his tuned Lyre, and wel accorded voyce, giueth praife, the reward of vertue, to vertuous acts? who giues morrall precepts, and naturall Problemes, who fometimes rayfeth vp his voice to the height of the heauens, in finging the laudes of the immortall God. Certainly I muft confeffe my own barbaroufnes, I neuer heard the olde song of *Percy* and *Duglas*, that I found not my heart mooued more then with a Trumpet : and yet is it fung but by fome blinde Crouder, with no rougher voyce, then rude ftile : which being fo euill apparrelled in the duft and cob-webbes of that vnciuill age, what would it worke trymmed in the gorgeous eloquence of *Pindar?* In *Hungary* I haue feene it the manner at all Feafts, and other fuch meetings, to haue fonges of their Aun-ceftours valour ; which that right Souldier-like Nation thinck the chiefeft kindlers of braue courage. The incomparable *Lacedemonians*, did not only carry that kinde of Muficke euer with them to the field, but euen at home, as fuch fongs were made, fo were they all content to bee the fingers of them, when the lufty men were to tell what they dyd, the olde men, what they had done, and the young men what they wold doe And where a man may fay, that *Pindar* many times prayfeth highly victories of fmall moment, matters rather of fport then vertue : as it may be aunfwered, it was the fault of the Poet, and not of the Poetry ; fo indeede, the chiefe fault was in the tyme and cuftome of the Greekes, who fet thofe toyes at fo high a price, that *Phillip* of *Macedon* reckoned a horfe-race wonne at *Olimpus*, among hys three fearefull felicities. But as the vnimitable *Pindar* often did, fo is that kinde moft capable and moft fit, to awake the thoughts from the fleep of idlenes, to imbrace honorable enter-prifes.

There refts the Heroicall, whofe very name (I thinke) fhould daunt all back-biters ; for by what conceit can a tongue be directed to fpeake euill of that, which draweth with it, no leffe Champions

then *Achilles, Cyrus, Aeneas, Turnus, Tideus,* and
Rinaldo? who doth not onely teach and moue to a
truth, but teacheth and mooueth to the moſt high and
excellent truth. VVho maketh magnanimity and iuſ-
tice ſhine, throughout all miſty fearefulnes and foggy
deſires. VVho, if the ſaying of *Plato* and *Tullie* bee
true, that who could ſee Vertue, would be wonderfully
rauiſhed with the loue of her beauty : this man ſets
her out to make her more louely in her holyday
apparell, to the eye of any that will daine, not to diſ-
daine, vntill they vnderſtand. But if any thing be
already ſayd in the defence of ſweete Poetry, all con-
curreth to the maintaining the Heroicall, which is not
onely a kinde, but the beſt, and moſt accompliſhed
kinde of Poetry. For as the image of each action
ſtyrreth and inſtructeth the mind, ſo the loftie image
of ſuch VVorthies, moſt inflameth the mind with deſire
to be worthy, and informes with counſel how to be
worthy. Only let *Aeneas* be worne in the tablet
of your memory, how he gouerneth himſelfe in the
ruine of his Country, in the preſeruing his old Father,
and carrying away his religious ceremonies : in obey-
ing the Gods commandement to leaue *Dido,* though
not onely all paſſionate kindenes, but euen the
humane conſideration of vertuous gratefulnes, would
haue craued other of him. How in ſtorms, howe in
ſports, howe in warre, howe in peace, how a fugitiue,
how victorious, how beſiedged, how beſiedging, howe
to ſtrangers, howe to allyes, how to enemies, howe to
his owne : laſtly, how in his inward ſelfe, and how in his
outward gouernment. And I thinke, in a minde not
preiudiced with a preiudicating humor, hee will be found
in excellencie fruitefull : yea, euen as *Horace* ſayth
    Melius Chriſippo et Crantore.
But truely I imagine, it falleth out with theſe Poet-
whyppers, as with ſome good women, who often are
ſicke, but in ſayth they cannot tel where. So the
name of Poetrie is odious to them, but neither his
cauſe, nor effects, neither the ſum that containes him,

nor the particularities defcending from him, giue any faft handle to their carping difprayfe.

Sith then Poetrie is of all humane learning the moft auncient, and of moft fatherly antiquitie, as from whence other learnings haue taken theyr beginnings : fith it is fo vniuerfall, that no learned Nation dooth defpife it, nor no barbarous Nation is without it : fith both Roman and Greek gaue diuine names vnto it : the one of prophecying, the other of making. And that indeede, that name of making is fit for him ; confidering, that where as other Arts retaine themfelues within their fubieĉt, and receiue as it were, their beeing from it : the Poet onely, bringeth his owne ftuffe, and dooth not learne a conceite out of a matter, but maketh matter for a conceite : Sith neither his defcription, nor his ende, contayneth any euill, the thing defcribed cannot be euill : Sith his effeĉts be fo good as to teach goodnes and to delight the learners : Sith therein, (namely in morrall doctrine, the chiefe of all knowledges,) hee dooth not onely farre paffe the Hiftorian, but for inftruĉting, is well nigh comparable to the Philofopher : and for mouing, leaues him behind him : Sith the holy fcripture (wherein there is no vncleannes) hath whole parts in it poeticall. And that euen our Sauiour Chrift, vouchfafed to vfe the flowers of it : Sith all his kindes are not onlie in their vnited formes, but in their feuered diffeĉtions fully commendable, I think, (and think I thinke rightly) the Lawrell crowne appointed for tryumphing Captaines, doth worthilie (of al other learnings) honor the Poets tryumph. But becaufe wee haue eares afwell as tongues, and that the lighteft reafons that may be, will feeme to weigh greatly, if nothing be put in the counter-ballance : let vs heare, and afwell as wee can ponder, what obieĉtions may bee made againft this Arte, which may be worthy, eyther of yeelding, or anfwering.

Firft truely I note, not onely in thefe *Myfomoufoi* Poet-haters. but in all that kinde of people, who feek

a prayfe by difprayfing others, that they doe prodi-.
gally fpend a great many wandering wordes, in quips,
and fcoffes; carping and taunting at each thing,
which by ftyrring the Spleene, may ftay the braine
from a through beholding the worthines of the
fubiect.

Thofe kinde of obiections, as they are full of very
idle eafines, fith there is nothing of fo facred a maieftie, but that an itching tongue may rubbe it felfe
vpon it : fo deferue they no other anfwer, but in fteed
of laughing at the ieft, to laugh at the iefter. VVee
know a playing wit, can prayfe the difcretion of an
Affe; the comfortablenes of being in debt, and the
iolly commoditie of beeing fick of the plague. So of
the contrary fide, if we will turne *Ouids* verfe,

Vt lateat virtus, proximitate mali,

that good lye hid in neereneffe of the euill : *Agrippa*
will be as merry in fhewing the vanitie of Science, as
Erafmus was in commending of follie. Neyther fhall
any man or matter efcape fome touch of thefe fmyling
raylers. But for *Erafmus* and *Agrippa*, they had
another foundation then the superficiall part would
promife. Mary, thefe other pleafant Fault-finders,
who wil correct the Verbe, before they vnderftande
the Noune, and confute others knowledge before
they confirme theyr owne : I would haue them onely
remember, that fcoffing commeth not of wifedom. So
as the beft title in true Englifh they gette with their
merriments, is to be called good fooles : for fo haue
our graue Fore-fathers euer termed that humorous
kinde of iefters : but that which gyueth greateft fcope
to their fcorning humors, is ryming and verfing. It
is already fayde (and as I think, trulie fayde) it is not
ryming and verfing, that maketh Poefie. One may
bee a Poet without verfing, and a verfifier without
Poetry. But yet, prefuppofe it were infeparable (as
indeede it feemeth *Scaliger* iudgeth) truelie it were an
infeparable commendation. For if *Oratio*, next to
Ratio, Speech next to Reafon, bee the greateft gyft

D

beſtowed vpon mortalitie: that can not be praiſeleſſe, which dooth moſt polliſh that bleſsing of ſpeech, which conſiders each word, not only (as a man may ſay) by his forcible qualitie, but by his beſt meaſured quantitie, carrying euen in themſelues, a Harmonie: (without (perchaunce) Number, Meaſure, Order, Proportion, be in our time growne odious.) But lay a ſide the iuſt prayſe it hath, by beeing the onely fit ſpeech for Muſick, (Muſick I ſay, the moſt diuine ſtriker of the ſences:) thus much is vndoubtedly true, that if reading bee fooliſh, without remembring, memorie being the onely treaſurer of knowled[g]e, those words which are fitteſt for memory, are likewiſe moſt conuenient for knowledge.

Now, that Verſe farre exceedeth Proſe in the knitting vp of the memory, the reaſon is manifeſt. The words, (beſides theyr delight which hath a great affinitie to memory,) beeing ſo ſet, as one word cannot be loſt, but the whole worke failes: which accuſeth it ſelfe, calleth the remembrance backe to it ſelfe, and ſo moſt ſtrongly confirmeth it; beſides, one word ſo as it were begetting another, as be it in ryme or meaſured verſe, by the former a man ſhall haue a neere geſſe to the follower: laſtly, euen they that haue taught the Art of memory, haue ſhewed nothing ſo apt for it, as a certaine roome deuided into many places well and throughly knowne. Now, that hath the verſe in effect perfectly: euery word hauing his naturall ſeate, which ſeate, muſt needes make the words remembred. But what needeth more in a thing ſo knowne to all men? who is it that euer was a ſcholler, that doth not carry away ſome verſes of *Virgill*, *Horace*, or *Cato*, which in his youth he learned, and euen to his old age ſerue him for howrely leſſons? but the fitnes it hath for memory, is notably proued by all deliuery of Arts: wherein for the moſt part, from Grammer, to Logick, Mathematick, Phiſick, and the reſt, the rules chiefely neceſſary to bee borne away, are compiled in verſes. So that, verſe being in it ſelfe ſweete and orderly, and beeing beſt for memory, the

onely handle of knowledge, it muſt be in ieſt that any
man can ſpeake againſt it. Nowe then goe wee to
the moſt important imputations laid to the poore
Poets, for ought I can yet learne, they are theſe, firſt,
that there beeing many other more fruitefull know-.
ledges, a man might better ſpend his tyme in them,
then in this. Secondly, that it is the mother of lyes.
Thirdly, that it is the Nurſe of abuſe, infecting vs with
many peſtilent deſires : with a Syrens ſweetnes, draw-,
ing the mind to the Serpents tayle of ſinfull fancy.,
And heerein eſpecially, Comedies giue the largeſt
field to erre, as *Chaucer* ſayth : howe both in other
Nations and in ours, before Poets did ſoften vs, we
were full of courage, giuen to martiall exerciſes ; the
pillers of manlyke liberty, and not lulled a ſleepe in
ſhady idlenes with Poets paſtimes. And · laſtly, and
chiefely, they cry out with an open mouth, as if they
out ſhot *Robin Hood*, that *Plato* baniſhed them out of
hys Common-wealth. Truely, this is much, if there
be much truth in it. Firſt to the firſt : that a man
might better ſpend his tyme, is a reaſon indeede : but
it doth (as they ſay) but *Petere principium* : for if it be
as I affirme, that no learning is ſo good, as that which
teacheth and mooueth to vertue ; and that none can
both teach and moue thereto ſo much as Poetry :
then is the concluſion manifeſt, that Incke and Paper
cannot be to a more profitable purpoſe employed.
And certainly, though a man ſhould graunt their firſt
aſſumption, it ſhould followe (me thinkes) very unwill-
ingly, that good is not good, becauſe better is better.
But I ſtill and vtterly denye, that there is ſprong out
of earth a more fruitefull knowledge. To the ſecond
therefore, that they ſhould be the principall lyars ; I
aunſwere paradoxically, but truely, I thinke truely ; that
of all VVriters vnder the ſunne, the Poet is the leaſt
lier : and though he would, as a Poet can ſcarcely be
a lyer, the Aſtronomer, with his coſen the Geometrician, can hardly eſcape, when they take vpon them to
meaſure the height of the ſtarres.

How often, thinke you, doe the Phifitians lye, wnen
they auer things, good for ficknefſes, which afterwards
fend *Charon* a great nomber of foules drown[e]d in a
potion before they come to his Ferry. And no lefſe of
the reſt, which take vpon them to affirme. Now, for
the Poet, he nothing affirmes, and therefore neuer
lyeth. For, as I take it, to lye, is to affirme that to be
true which is falfe. So as the other Artiſts, and efpecially the Hiſtorian, affirming many things, can in the
cloudy knowledge of mankinde, hardly efcape from
many lyes. But the Poet as (I fayd before) neuer
affirmeth. The Poet neuer maketh any circles about
your imagination, to coniure you to beleeue for true
what he writes. Hee citeth not authorities of other
Hiſtories, but euen for hys entry, calleth the fweete
Mufes to infpire into him a good inuention : in troth,
not labouring to tell you what is, or is not, but what
fhould or fhould not be : and therefore, though he recount things not true, yet becaufe hee telleth them not
for true, he lyeth not, without we will fay, that *Nathan*,
lyed in his fpeech, before alledged to *Dauid.* VVhich
as a wicked man durſt fcarce fay, fo think I, none fo
fimple would fay, that *Efope* lyed in the tales of his
beaſts : for who thinks that *Efope* writ it for actually
true, were well worthy to haue his name c[h]ronicled
among the beaſtes hee writeth of.

    · VVhat childe is there, that comming to a Play, and
feeing *Thebes* written in great Letters vpon an olde
doore, doth beleeue that it is *Thebes?* If then, a man
can ariue, at that childs age, to know that the Poets
perfons and dooings, are but pictures what fhould be,
and not ſtories what haue beene, they will neuer giue
the lye, to things not affirmatiuely, but allegorically,
and figuratiuelie written. And therefore, as in Hiſtorie,
looking for trueth, they goe away full fraught with falf-
hood : fo in Poefie, looking for fiction, they fhal vfe
the narration, but as an imaginatiue groundplot of a
profitable inuention.

    But heereto is replyed, that the Poets gyue names

to men they write of, which argueth a conceite of an
actuall truth, and so, not being true, prooues a falshood.
And doth the Lawyer lye then, when vnder the names
of *Iohn a stile* and *Iohn a noakes*, hee puts his cafe?
But that is eafily anfwered. Theyr naming of men, is
but to make theyr picture the more liuely, and not to
builde any hiftorie : paynting men, they cannot leaue
men namelesse. VVe fee we cannot play at Cheffe, but
that wee muft giue names to our Cheffe-men ; and yet
mee thinks, hee were a very partiall Champion of truth,
that would fay we lyed, for giuing a peece of wood, the
reuerend title of a Bifhop. The Poet nameth *Cyrus*
or *Aeneas*, no other way, then to fhewe, what men of
theyr fames, fortunes, and eftates, fhould doe.

Their third is, how much it abufeth mens wit, trayn-
ing it to wanton finfulnes, and luftfull loue : for indeed
that is the principall, if not the onely abufe I can heare
alledged. They fay, the Comedies rather teach, then
reprehend, amorous conceits. They fay, the Lirick, is
larded with pafsionate Sonnets. The Elegiack, weepes
the want of his miftreffe. And that euen to the Hero-
ical, *Cupid* hath ambitioufly climed. Alas Loue, I
would, thou couldeft as well defende thy felfe, as thou
canft offende others. I would thofe, on whom thou
dooft attend, could eyther put thee away, or yeelde
good reafon, why they keepe thee. But grant loue of
beautie, to be a beaftlie fault, (although it be very hard,
fith onely man, and no beaft, hath that gyft, to difcerne
beauty.) Grant, that louely name of Loue, to deferue
all hatefull reproches: (although euen fome of my
Maifters the Phylofophers, fpent a good deale of theyr
Lamp-oyle, in fetting foorth the excellencie of it.)
Grant, I fay, what foeuer they wil haue granted ; that
not onely loue, but luft, but vanitie, but, (if they lift)
fcurrilitie, poffeffeth many leaues of the Poets bookes :
yet thinke I, when this is granted, they will finde, theyr
fentence may with good manners, put the laft words
foremoft : and not fay, that Poetrie abufeth mans wit,
but that, mans wit abufeth Poetrie.

For I will not denie, but that mans wit may make Poefie, (which fhould be *Eikaſtike*, which fome learned haue defined, figuring foorth good things,) to be *Phantaſtike:* which doth contrariwife, infect the fancie with vnworthy obiects. As the Painter, that fhoulde giue to the eye, eyther fome excellent perfpectiue, or fome fine picture, fit for building or fortification : or contayning in it fome notable example, as *Abraham,* facrificing his Sonne *Iſaack, Iudith* killing *Holofernes, Dauid* fighting with *Goliah,* may leaue thofe, and pleafe an ill-pleafed eye, with wanton fhewes of better hidden matters. But what, fhall the abufe of a thing, make the right vfe odious? Nay truely, though I yeeld, that Poefie may not onely be abufed, but that beeing abufed, by the reafon of his fweete charming force, it can doe more hurt then any other Armie of words : yet fhall it be fo far from concluding, that the abufe, fhould giue reproch to the abufed, that contrari-wife it is a good reafon, that whatfoeuer being abufed, dooth moſt harme, beeing rightly vfed : (and vpon the right vfe each thing conceiueth his title) doth moſt good.

Doe wee not fee the fkill of Phiſick, (the beſt rampire to our often-affaulted bodies) beeing abufed, teach poyfon the moſt violent deſtroyer? Dooth not knowledge of Law, whofe end is, to euen and right all things being abufed, grow the crooked foſterer of horrible iniuries? Doth not (to goe to the higheſt) Gods word abufed, breed herefie? and his Name abufed, become blafphemie? Truely, a needle cannot doe much hurt, and as truely, (with leaue of Ladies be it fpoken) it cannot doe much good. With a fword, thou maiſt kill thy Father, and with a fword thou maiſt defende thy Prince and Country. So that, as in their calling Poets the Fathers of lyes, they say nothing : fo in this theyr argument of abufe, they prooue the commendation.

They alledge heere-with, that before Poets beganne to be in price, our Nation, hath fet their harts delight vpon action, and not vpon imagination : rather doing

things worthy to bee written, then writing things fitte
to be done. VVhat that before tyme was, I thinke
fcarcely *Sphinx* can tell : Sith no memory is fo auncient,
that hath the precedence of Poetrie. And certaine
it is, that in our plaineft homelines, yet neuer was
the *Albion* Nation without Poetrie. Mary, thys argument, though it bee leaueld againft Poetrie, yet is it
indeed, a chaine-fhot againft all learning, or book-
ifhnes, as they commonly tearme it. Of fuch minde
were certaine *Gothes*, of whom it is written, that
hauing in the fpoile of a famous Citie, taken a fayre
librarie : one hangman (bee like fitte to execute the
fruites of their wits) who had murthered a great
number of bodies, would haue fet fire on it : no fayde
another, very grauely, take heede what you doe, for
whyle they are bufie about thefe toyes, wee fhall with
more leyfure conquer their Countries.

This indeede is the ordinary doctrine of ignorance,
and many wordes fometymes I haue heard fpent in
it : but becaufe this reafon is generally againftall
learning, afwell as Poetrie ; or rather, all learning but
Poetry : becaufe it were too large a digrefsion, to handle, or at leaft, to fuperfluous : (fith it is manifeft,
that all gouernment of action, is to be gotten by know-
ledg, and knowledge beft, by gathering many knowledges, which is, reading,) I onely with *Horace*, to him
that is of that opinion,
        Iubeo ftultum efte libenter :
for as for Poetrie it felfe, it is the freeft from thys ob-
iection. For Poetrie is the companion of the Campes.

I dare vndertake, *Orlando Furiofo*, or honeft King
Arthur, will neuer difpleafe a Souldier : but the quid-
dity of *Ens*, and *Prima materia*, will hardely agree
with a Corflet : and therefore, as I faid in the beginning, euen Turks and Tartares are delighted with
Poets. *Homer* a Greek, florifhed, before Greece
florifhed. And if to a flight coniecture, a coniecture
may be oppofed : truly it may feeme, that as by him,
their learned men, tooke almoft their firft light of

knowledge, fo their actiue men, receiued their firft
motions of courage. Onlie *Alexanders* example may
ferue, who by *Plutarch* is accounted of fuch vertue,
that Fortune was not his guide, but his foote-ftoole:
whofe acts fpeake for him, though *Plutarch* did not:
indeede, the Phœnix of warlike Princes. This *Alexander*, left his Schoolemaifter, liuing *Ariftotle*, behinde
him, but tooke deade *Homer* with him : he put the
Philofopher *Califthenes* to death, for his feeming philofophicall, indeed mutinous ftubburnnes. But the chiefe
thing he euer was heard to wifh for, was, that *Homer*
had been aliue. He well found, he receiued more
brauerie of minde, bye the patterne of *Achilles*, then
by hearing the definition of Fortitude: and therefore,
if *Cato* mifliked *Fuluius*, for carying *Ennius* with him
to the fielde, it may be aunfwered, that if *Cato* mifliked
it, the noble *Fuluius* liked it, or els he had not doone
it: for it was not the excellent *Cato Vticenfis*, (whofe
authority I would much more haue reuerenced,) but
it was the former: in truth, a bitter punifher of faults,
but elfe, a man that had neuer wel facrificed to the
Graces. Hee mifliked and cryed out vpon all Greeke
learning, and yet being 80. yeeres olde, began to
learne it. Be-like, fearing that *Pluto* vnderftood not
Latine. Indeede, the Romaine lawes allowed, no
perfon to be carried to the warres, but hee that was
in the Souldiers role : and therefore, though *Cato*
mifliked his vnmuftered perfon, hee mifliked not his
worke. And if hee had, *Scipio Nafica* iudged by common confent, the beft Romaine, loued him. Both the
other *Scipio* Brothers, who had by their vertues no
leffe furnames, then of *Afia*, and *Affrick*, fo loued him,
that they caufed his body to be buried in their Sepul-
cher. So as *Cato*, his authoritie being but againft his
perfon, and that aunfwered, with fo farre greater then
himfelfe, is heerein of no validitie. But now indeede
my burthen is great ; now *Plato* his name is layde
vpon mee, whom I muft confeffe, of all Philofophers,
I haue euer efteemed moft worthy of reuerence, and

with great reafon : Sith of all Philofophers, he is the
moft poeticall. Yet if he will defile the Fountaine,
out of which his flowing ftreames haue proceeded, let
vs boldly examine with what reafons hee did it. Firft
truly, a man might malicioufly obiect, that *Plato* being
a Philofopher, was a naturall enemie of Poets : for
indeede, after the Philofophers, had picked out of the
fweete mifteries of Poetrie, the right difcerning true
points of knowledge, they forthwith putting it in
method, and making a Schoole-arte of that which the
Poets did onely teach, by a diuine delightfulnes, beginning to fpurne at their guides, like vngratefull Prentifes,
were not content to fet vp fhops for themfelues, but
fought by all meanes to difcredit their Maifters.
VVhich by the force of delight beeing barred them, the
leffe they could ouerthrow them, the more they hated
them. For indeede, they found for *Homer*, feauen Cities
ftroue, who fhould haue him for their Citizen : where
many Citties banifhed Philofophers, as not fitte mem-
bers to liue among them. For onely repeating certaine
of *Euripides* verfes, many *Athenians* had their lyues
faued of the *Siracufians* : when the *Athenians* themfelues, thought many Philofophers, vnwoorthie to liue.
  Certaine Poets, as *Simonides*, and *Pindarus* had fo
preuailed with *Hiero* the firft, that of a Tirant they
made him a iuft King, where *Plato* could do fo little
with *Dionifius*, that he himfelfe, of a Philofopher, was
made a flaue. But who should doe thus, I confeffe,
fhould requite the obiections made againft Poets,
with like cauillation againft Philofophers, as likewife
one fhould doe, that fhould bid one read *Phædrus*, or
Sympofium in *Plato*, or the difcourfe of loue in *Plutarch*, and fee whether any Poet doe authorize abhominable filthines, as they doe. Againe, a man might aske
out of what Common-wealth *Plato* did banifh them ?
infooth, thence where he himfelfe alloweth communi-
tie of women : So as belike, this banifhment grewe
not for effeminate wantonnes, fith little should poeticall Sonnets be hurtfull, when a man might haue what

woman he lifted. But I honor philofophicall inftructions, and bleffe the wits which bred them : fo as they be not abufed, which is likewife ftretched to Poetrie. S. *Paule* himfelfe, (who yet for the credite of Poets) alledgeth twife two Poets, and one of them by the name of a Prophet, fetteth a watch-word vpon Philofophy, indeede vpon the abufe. So dooth *Plato*, vpon the abufe, not vpon Poetrie. *Plato* found fault, that the Poets of his time, filled the worlde, with wrong opinions of the Gods, making light tales of that vnfpotted effence ; and therefore, would not haue the youth depraued with fuch opinions. Heerin may much be faid, let this fuffice : the Poets did not induce fuch opinions, but dyd imitate thofe opinions already induced. For all the Greek ftories can well teftifie, that the very religion of that time, ftoode vpon many, and many-fafhioned Gods, not taught fo by the Poets, but followed, according to their nature of imitation. VVho lift, may reade in *Plutarch*, the difcourfes of *Ifis*, and *Ofiris*, of the caufe why Oracles ceafed, of the diuine prouidence : and fee, whether the Theologie of that nation, ftood not vpon fuch dreames, which the Poets indeed fuperfticioufly obferued, and truly, (fith they had not the light of Chrift,) did much better in it then the Philofophers, who fhaking off fuperftition, brought in Atheifme. *Plato* therefore, (whofe authoritie I had much rather iuftly confter, then uniuftly refift,) meant not in general of Poets, in thofe words of which *Iulius Scaliger* faith *Qua authoritate, barbari quidam, atque hifpidi, abuti velint, ad Poetas é republica exigendos :* but only meant, to driue out thofe wrong opinions of the Deitie (whereof now, without further law, Chriftianity hath taken away all the hurtful beliefe,) perchance (as he thought) norifhed by the then efteemed Poets. And a man need goe no further then to *Plato* himfelfe, to know his meaning : who in his Dialogue called *Ion*, giueth high, and rightly diuine commendation to Poetrie. So as *Plato*, banifhing the abufe, not the thing, not banifhing it,

but giuing due honor vnto it, fhall be our Patron, and
not our aduerfarie. For indeed I had much rather,
(fith truly I may doe it) fhew theyr miftaking of *Plato*,
(vnder whofe Lyons fkin they would make an Affe-
like braying againft Poefie,) then goe about to ouerthrow his authority, whom the wifer a man is, the
more iuft caufe he fhall find to haue in admiration:
efpecially, fith he attributeth vnto Poefie, more then
my felfe doe; namely, to be a very infpiring of a
diuine force, farre aboue mans wit; as in the afore-
named Dialogue is apparant.

Of the other fide, who wold fhew the honors, haue
been by the beft fort of iudgements granted them, a
whole Sea of examples woulde prefent themfelues.
Alexanders, *Cæfars*, *Scipios*, al fauorers of Poets.
Lelius, called the Romane *Socrates*, himfelfe a Poet:
fo as part of *Heautontimorumenon* in *Terence*, was fup-
pofed to be made by him. And euen the Greek
Socrates, whom *Apollo* confirmed to be the onely wife
man, is fayde to haue fpent part of his old tyme, in
putting *Efops* fables into verfes. And therefore, full
euill fhould it become his fcholler *Plato*, to put fuch
words in his Maifters mouth, againft Poets. But what
need more? *Ariftotle* writes the Arte of Poefie: and
why if it fhould not be written? *Plutarch* teacheth
the vfe to be gathered of them, and how if they fhould
not be read? And who reades *Plutarchs* eyther hiftorie or philofophy, fhall finde, hee trymmeth both
theyr garments, with gards of Poefie. But I lift not
to defend Poefie, with the helpe of her vnderling,
Hiftoriography. Let it fuffife, that it is a fit foyle for
prayfe to dwell vpon: and what difpraife may fet vpon
it, is eyther eafily ouer-come, or transformed into iuft
commendation. So that, fith the excellencies of it,
may be fo eafily, and fo iuftly confirmed, and the low-
creeping obiections, fo foone troden downe; it not
being an Art of lyes, but of true doctrine: not of
effeminatenes, but of notable ftirring of courage: not
of abufing mans witte, but of ftrengthning mans wit:

not banifhed, but honored by *Plato* : let vs rather
plant more Laurels, for to engarland our Poets heads,
(which honor of beeing laureat, as befides them, onely
tryumphant Captaines weare, is a fufficient authority,
to fhewe the price they ought to be had in,) then
fuffer the ill-fauouring breath of fuch wrong-fpeakers,
once to blowe vpon the cleere fprings of Poefie.

But fith I have runne fo long a careere in this
matter, me thinks, before I giue my penne a fulle
ftop, it fhalbe but a little more loft time, to in-
quire, why England, (the Mother of excellent mindes,)
fhould bee growne fo hard a ftep-mother to Poets, vvho
certainly in wit ought to paffe all other : fith all onely
proceedeth from their wit, being indeede makers of themfelues, not takers of others.   How can I but exclaime,
Mufa mihi caufas memora, quo numine læfo.
Sweete Poefie, that hath aunciently had Kings,
Emperors, Senators, great Captaines, fuch, as be-
fides a thoufand others, *Dauid*, *Adrian*, *Sophocles*,
Germanicus, not onely to fauour Poets, but to be
Poets.   And of our neerer times, can prefent for her
Patrons, a *Robert*, king of Sicil, the great king
Francis of France, King *Iames* of Scotland.   Such
Cardinals as *Bembus*, and *Bibiena*.   Such famous
Preachers and Teachers, as *Beza* and *Melančlhon*.
So learned Philofophers, as *Fracaflorius* and *Scaliger*.
So great Orators, as *Pontanus* and *Muretus*.   So
piercing wits, as *George Buchanan*.   So graue Coun-
fellors, as befides many, but before all, that *Hofpitali*
of Fraunce : then whom, (I thinke) that Realme
neuer brought forth a more accomplifhed iudgement :
more firmely builded vpon vertue.   I fay thefe, with
numbers of others, not onely to read others Poefies,
but to poetife for others reading, that Poefie thus em-
braced in all other places, fhould onely finde in our time,
a hard welcome in England, I thinke the very earth
lamenteth it, and therfore decketh our Soyle with
fewer Laurels then it was accuftomed.   For heerto-
fore, Poets haue in England alfo florifhed.   And which

is to be noted, euen in thofe times, when the trumpet
of *Mars* did founde loudeſt. And now, that an ouer-
faint quietnes fhould feeme to ſtrew the houfe for
Poets, they are almoſt in as good reputation, as the
Mountibancks at *Venice.* Truly euen that, as of the
one fide, it giueth great praife to Poefie, which like
Venus, (but to better purpofe) hath rather be troubled
in the net with *Mars*, then enioy the homelie quiet
of *Vulcan* : fo ferues it for a peece of a reafon, why
they are leffe gratefull to idle England, which nowe,
can fcarce endure the payne of a pen. Vpon this,
neceffarily followeth, that bafe men, with feruile wits
vndertake it : who think it inough, if they can be
rewarded of the Printer. And fo as *Epaminondas* is
fayd, with the honor of his vertue, to haue made an
office, by his exercifing it, which before was con-
temptible, to become highly refpected : fo thefe, no
more but fetting their names to it, by their owne dif-
gracefulnes, difgrace the moſt gracefull Poefie. For
now, as if all the Mufes were gotte with childe, to
bring foorth baſtard Poets, without any commifsion,
they doe poſte ouer the banckes of *Helicon*, tyll they
make the readers more weary then Poſt-horfes : while
in the mean tyme, they

Queis meliore luto finxit præcordia Titan,

are better content, to fuppreffe the out-flowing of their
wit, then by publifhing them, to bee accounted Knights
of the same order. But I, that before euer I durſt afpire
vnto the dignitie, am admitted into the company of
the Paper-blurers, doe finde the very true caufe of our
wanting eſtimation, is want of defert : taking vpon vs
to be Poets, in defpight of *Pallas.* Nowe, wherein
we want defert, were a thanke-worthy labour to expreffe : but if I knew, I fhould haue mended my felfe.
But I, as I neuer defired the title, fo haue I neglected
the meanes to come by it. Onely ouer-maſtred by
fome thoughts, I yeelded an inckie tribute vnto them.
Mary, they that delight in Poefie it felfe, fhould feeke
to knowe what they doe, and how they doe ; and

efpecially, looke themfelues in an vnflattering Glaffe of reafon, if they bee inclinable vnto it. For Poefie, muft not be drawne by the eares, it muft bee gently led, or rather, it muft lead. VVhich was partly the caufe, that made the auncient-learned affirme, it was a diuine gift, and no humaine skill : fith all other knowledges, lie ready for any that hath ftrength of witte : A Poet, no induftrie can make, if his owne *Genius* bee not carried vnto it : and therefore is it an old Prouerbe, *Orator fit; Poeta nafcitur.* Yet confeffe I alwayes, that as the firtileft ground muft bee manured, so muft the higheft flying wit, have a *Dedalus* to guide him. That *Dedalus,* they fay, both in this, and in other, hath three wings, to beare it felfe vp into the ayre of due commendation : that is, Arte, Imitation, and Exercife. But thefe, neyther artificiall rules, nor imitatiue patternes, we much cumber our felues withall. Exercife indeede wee doe, but that, very fore-backwardly : for where we should exercife to know, wee exercife as hauing knowne : and fo is oure braine deliuered of much matter, which neuer was begotten by knowledge. For, there being two principal parts, matter to be expreffed by wordes, and words to expreffe the matter, in neyther, wee vfe Arte, or Imitation, rightly. Our matter is *Quodlibit* indeed, though wrongly perfourming *Ouids* verfe.

(*Quicquid conabar dicere verfus erit* :)

neuer marfhalling it into an affured rancke, that almoft the readers cannot tell where to finde themfelues.

Chaucer, vndoubtedly did excellently in hys *Troylus* and *Creffeid*; of whom, truly I know not, whether to meruaile more, either that he in that miftie time, could fee fo clearely, or that wee in this cleare age, walke fo ftumblingly after him. Yet had he great wants, fitte to be forgiuen, in fo reuerent antiquity. I account the *Mirrour of Magiftrates,* meetely furnifhed of beautiful parts ; and in the Earle of Surries *Liricks,* many things tafting of a noble birth, and worthy of a noble minde. The *Sheapheards Kalender,* hath much Poetrie in his Eglogues : indeede worthy the reading if I be not deceiued. That fame framing of his ftile, to an old ruftick language, I dare not alowe, fith neyther *Theocritus* in Greeke, *Virgill* in Latine, nor *Sanazar* in Italian, did affect it. Befides thefe, doe I not remember to haue feene but fewe, (to fpeake boldely) printed, that haue poeticall finnewes in them: for proofe whereof, let but moft of the verfes bee put in Profe, and then aske the meaning; and it will be found, that one verfe did but beget another, without ordering at the firft, what fhould be at the laft: which becomes a confufed maffe of words, with a tingling found of ryme, barely accompanied with reafon.

Our Tragedies, and Comedies, (not without caufe. cried out againft,) obferuing rules, neyther of honeft ciuilitie, nor of fkilfull Poetrie, excepting *Gorboduck*, (againe, I fay, of thofe that I haue feene,) which notwithftanding, as it is full of ftately fpeeches, and well founding Phrafes, clyming to the height of *Seneca* his ftile, and as full of notable moralitie, which it doth moft delightfully teach; and fo obtayne the very end of Poefie: yet in troth it is very defectious in the circumftaunces; which greeueth mee, becaufe it might not remaine as an exact model of all Tragedies. For it is faulty both in place, and time, the two neceffary companions of all corporall actions. For where the ftage fhould alwaies reprefent but one place, and the vttermoft time prefuppofed in it, fhould be, both by *Ariftotles* precept, and common reafon, but one day: there is both many dayes, and many places, inartificially imagined. But if it be fo in *Gorboduck*, how much more in al the reft? where you fhal haue *Afia* of the one fide, and *Affrick* of the other, and fo many other vnder-kingdoms, that the Player, when he commeth in, muft euer begin with telling where he is: or els, the tale wil not be conceiued. Now ye fhal haue three Ladies, walke to gather flowers, and then we muft beleeue the ftage to be a Garden. By and by, we heare newes of fhipwracke in the fame place, and then wee are to blame, if we accept it not for a Rock.

Vpon the backe of that, comes out a hidious Mon-
fter, with fire and fmoke, and then the miferable
beholders, are bounde to take it for a Caue.   VVhile
in the mean-time, two Armies flye in, reprefented
with foure fwords and bucklers, and then what harde
heart will not receiue it for a pitched fielde ?   Now,
of time they are much more liberall, for ordinary it is
that two young Princes fall in loue.   After many
trauerces, fhe is got with childe, deliuered of a faire .
boy, he is loft, groweth a man, falls in loue, and is
ready to get another child, and all this in two hours
fpace : which how abfurd it is in fence, euen fence.
may imagine, and Arte hath taught, and all auncient
examples iuftified :   and at this day, the ordinary
Players in Italie, wil not erre in.   Yet wil fome bring
in an. example of *Eunuchus* in *Terence*, that containeth matter of two dayes, yet far fhort of twenty
yeeres.   True it is, and fo was it to be playd in two
daies, and fo fitted to the time it fet forth.   And though
Plautus hath in one place done amiffe, let vs hit with
him, and not miffe with him.   But they wil fay, how
then fhal we fet forth a ftory, which containeth both
many places, and many times ?   And doe they not
knowe, that a Tragedie is tied to the lawes of Poefie,
and not of Hiftorie ? not bound to follow the ftorie,
but hauing liberty, either to faine a quite newe matter, or to frame the hiftory, to the moft tragicall conueniencie.   Againe, many things may be told, which
cannot be fhewed, if they knowe the difference betwixt
reporting and reprefenting.   As for example, I may
fpeake, (though I am heere) of *Peru*, and in fpeech,
digreffe from that, to the defcription of *Calicut* : but
in action, I cannot reprefent it without *Pacolets* horfe :
and fo was the manner the Auncients tooke, by fome
Nuncius, to recount thinges done in former time, or
other place.   Laftly, if they wil reprefent an hiftory,
they muft not (as *Horace* faith) beginne *Ab ouo* : but
they muft come to the principall poynt of that one
action,. which they wil reprefent. By example this

wil be beſt expreſſed. I haue a ſtory of young *Poli-dorus*, deliuered for ſafeties ſake, with great riches, by his Father *Priamus* to *Polimneſtor* king of *Thrace*, in the Troyan war time : Hee after ſome yeeres, hearing the ouer-throwe of *Priamus*, for to make the treaſure his owne, murthereth the child : the body of the child is taken vp *Hecuba*, ſhee the ſame day, findeth a ſlight to bee reuenged moſt cruelly of the Tyrant: where nowe would one of our Tragedy writers begin, but with the deliuery of the childe ? Then ſhould he fayle ouer into *Thrace*, and ſo ſpend I know not how many yeeres, and trauaile numbers of places. But where dooth *Euripides?* Euen with the finding of the body, leauing the reſt to be tolde by the ſpirit of *Polidorus.* This need no further to be inlarged, the dulleſt wit may conceiue it. But beſides theſe groſſe abſurdities, how all theyr Playes be neither right Tragedies, nor right Comedies : mingling Kings and Clownes, not becauſe the matter ſo carrieth it : but thruſt in Clownes by head and ſhoulders, to play a part in maieſticall matters, with neither decencie nor diſcretion. So as neither the admiration and commiſeration, nor the right ſportfulnes, is by their mungrell Tragy-comedie obtained. I know *Apuleius* did ſome-what ſo, but that is a thing recounted with ſpace of time, not repreſented in one moment : and I knowe, the Auncients haue one or two examples of Tragy-comedies, as *Plautus* hath *Amphitrio* : But if we marke them well, we ſhall find, that they neuer, or very daintily, match Horn-pypes and Funeralls. So falleth it out, that hauing indeed no right Comedy, in that comicall part of our Tragedy, we haue nothing but ſcurrility, vnwoorthy of any chaſt eares : or ſome extreame ſhew of doltiſhnes, indeed fit to lift vp a loude laughter, and nothing els : where the whole tract of a Comedy, ſhoulde be full of delight, as the Tragedy ſhoulde be ſtill maintained, in a well raiſed admiration. But our Comedians, thinke there is no delight without laughter, which is very wrong, for

E

though laughter may come with delight, yet commeth it not of delight: as though delight fhould be the caufe of laughter, but well may one thing breed both together : nay, rather in themfelues, they haue as it were, a kind of contrarietie : for delight we fcarcely doe, but in things that haue a conueniencie to our felues, or to the generall nature : laughter, almoft euer commeth, of things moft difproportioned to our felues, and nature. Delight hath a ioy in it, either permanent, or prefent. Laughter, hath onely a fcornful tickling.

For example, we are rauifhed with delight to fee a faire woman, and yet are far from being moued to laughter. VVe laugh at deformed creatures, wherein certainely we cannot delight. VVe delight in good chaunces, we laugh at mifchaunces; we delight to heare the happines of our friends, or Country ; at which he were worthy to be laughed at, that would laugh ; wee fhall contrarily laugh fometimes, to finde a matter quite miftaken, and goe downe the hill agaynft the byas, in the mouth of fome fuch men, as for the refpect of them, one fhalbe hartely forry, yet he cannot chufe but laugh ; and fo is rather pained, then delighted with laughter. Yet deny I not, but that they may goe well together, for as in *Alexanders* picture vvell fet out, wee delight without laughter, and in twenty mad Anticks we laugh without delight: fo in *Hercules*, painted with his great beard, and furious countenance, in womans attire, fpinning at *Omphales* commaurdement, it breedeth both delight and laughter. For the reprefenting of fo ftrange a power in loue, procureth delight : and the fcornefulnes of the action, ftirreth laughter. But I fpeake to this purpofe, that all the end of the comicall part, bee not vpon fuch fcornefull matters, as ftirreth laughter onely : but mixt with it, that delightful teaching which is the end of Poefie. And the great fault euen in that point of laughter, and forbidden plainely by *Ariftotle*, is, that they ftyrre laughter in finfull things ; which are rather execrable then ridiculous : or in miferable, which are rather to be pittied than fcorned.

For what is it to make folkes gape at a wretched Beg-
ger, or a beggerly Clowne? or againſt lawe of hoſpitality,
to ieſt at ſtraungers, becauſe they ſpeake not Engliſh ſo
well as wee doe? what do we learne, ſith it is certaine
(*Nil habet infœlix paupertas durius in ſe,*)
Quam quod ridiculos homines facit.———
But rather a buſy louing Courtier, a hartles threatening
Thraſo. A ſelfe-wiſe-ſeeming ſchoolemaſter. A awry-
transformed Traueller. Theſe, if we ſawe walke in
ſtage names, which wee play naturally, therein were delightfull laughter, and teaching delightfulnes : as in the
other, the Tragedies of *Buchanan,* doe iuſtly bring
forth a diuine admiration. But I haue lauiſhed out
too many wordes of this play matter. I doe it becauſe
as they are excelling parts of Poeſie, ſo is there none
ſo much vſed in England, and none can be more pitti-
fully abuſed. VVhich like an vnmannerly Daughter,
ſhewing a bad education, cauſeth her mother Poeſies
honeſty, to bee called in queſtion. Other ſorts of Poetry
almoſt haue we none, but that Lyricall kind of Songs
and Sonnets : which, Lord, if he gaue vs ſo good
mindes, how well it might be imployed, and with howe
heauenly fruite, both priuate and publique, in ſinging
the prayſes of the immortall beauty : the immortall
goodnes of that God, who gyueth vs hands to write,
and wits to conceiue, of which we might well want
words, but neuer matter, of which, we could turne our
eies to nothing, but we ſhould euer haue new budding
occaſions. But truely many of ſuch writings, as come
vnder the banner of vnreſiſtable loue, if I were a
Miſtres, would neuer perſwade mee they were in loue :
ſo coldely they apply fiery ſpeeches, as men that had
rather red Louers writings ; and ſo caught vp certaine
ſwelling phraſes, which hang together, like a man   -
which once tolde mee, the winde was at North, VVeſt,
and by South, becauſe he would be ſure to name windes
enovve : then that in truth they feele thoſe paſsions,
which eaſily (as I think) may be bewrayed, by that ſame
forciblenes, or *Energia,* (as the Greekes cal it) of the

writer. But let this bee a fufficient, though fhort note, that wee miffe the right vfe of the materiall point of Poefie.

Now, for the out-fide of it, which is words, or (as I may tearme it) *Diction*, it is euen well worfe. So is that honny-flowing Matron Eloquence, apparelled, or rather difguifed, in a Curtizan-like painted affectation : one time with fo farre fette words, they may feeme Monfters: but muft feeme ftraungers to any poore Englifh man. Another tyme, with courfing of a Let-ter, as if they were bound to followe the method of a Dictionary : an other tyme, with figures and flowers, extreamelie winter-ftarued. But I would this fault were only peculier to Verfifiers, and had not as large poffeffion among Profe-printers ; and, (which is to be meruailed) among many Schollers ; and, (which is to be pittied) among fome Preachers. Truly I could wifh, if at leaft I might be fo bold, to wifh in a thing beyond the reach of my capacity, the diligent imita-tors of *Tullie*, and *Demofthenes*, (moft worthy to be imitated) did not fo much keep, *Nizolian* Paper-bookes of their figures and phrafes, as by attentiue tranflation (as it were) deuoure them whole, and make them wholly theirs : For nowe they caft Sugar and Spice, vpon euery difh that is ferued to the table ; Like thofe Indians, not content to weare eare-rings at the fit and naturall place of the eares, but they will thruft Iewels through their nofe, and lippes becaufe they will be fure to be fine.

Tullie, when he was to driue out *Cateline*, as it were with a Thunder-bolt of eloquence, often vied that figure of repitition, *Viuit viuit ? imo Senatum venit &c.* Indeed, inflamed with a well-grounded rage, hee would haue his words (as it were) double out of his mouth : and fo doe that artificially, which we fee men doe in choller naturally. And wee, hauing noted the grace of thofe words, hale them in fometime to a familier Epiftle, when it were to too much choller to be chollerick. Fow for fimilitudes, in certaine printed difcourfes, I thinke all Herbarifts, all ftories of Beafts, Foules, and Fifhes, are rifled vp, that they come in

multitudes, to waite vpon any of our conceits ; which
certainly is as abfurd a furfet to the eares, as is pofsible :
for the force of a fimilitude, not being to prooue any·
thing to a contrary Difputer, but onely to explane to a
willing hearer, when that is done, the reft is a moft
tedious pratling : rather ouer-fwaying the memory
from the purpofe whereto they were applyed, then
any whit informing the iudgement, already eyther fatis·
fied, or by fimilitudes not to be fatif-fied. For my
part, I doe not doubt, when *Antonius* and *Craffus,*
the great forefathers of *Cicero* in eloquence, the one
(as *Cicero* teftifieth of them) pretended not to know
Arte, the other, not to fet by it : becaufe with a playne
fenfiblenes, they might win credit of popular eares; which
credit, is the neereft ftep to perfwafion : which perfwafion,
is the chiefe marke of Oratory ; I doe not doubt (I fay)
but that they vfed thefe tracks very fparingly, which who
doth generally vfe, any man may fee doth daunce to
his owne mufick : and fo be noted by the audience,
more careful to fpeake curioufly, then to fpeake truly.

Vndoubtedly, (at leaft to my opinion vndoubtedly,)
I haue found in diuers fmally learned Courtiers, a more
founde ftile, then in some profeffors of learning: of which
I can geffe no other caufe, but that the Courtier following
that which by practife hee findeth fitteft to nature, therein, (though he know it not,) doth according to Art, though
not by Art : where the other, vfing Art to fhew Art, and
not to hide Art, (as in thefe cafes he fhould doe) flyeth
from nature, and indeede abufeth Art.

But what ? me thinkes I deferue to be pounded, foi
ftraying from Poetrie to Oratorie : but both haue fuch
an affinity in this wordifh confideration, that I thinke
this digrefsion, will make my meaning receiue the
fuller vnderftanding : which is not to take vpon me to
teach Poets hovve they fhould doe, but onely finding
my felfe fick among the reft, to fhewe fome one or
two fpots of the conimon infection, growne among the
moft part of VVriters : that acknowledging our felues
fomewhat awry, we may bend to the right vfe both of

matter and manner ; whereto our language gyueth vs great occafion, beeing indeed capable of any excellent exercifing of it.   I know, fome will fay it is a mingled language.   And why not fo much the better, taking the beft of both the other?   Another will fay it wanteth Grammer.   Nay truly, it hath that prayfe, that it wanteth not Grammer : for Grammer it might haue, but it needes it not; beeing so eafie of it felfe, and fo voyd of thofe cumberfome differences of Cafes, Genders, Moodes, and Tenfes, which I thinke was a peece of the Tower of *Babilons* curfe, that a man fhould be put to fchoole to learne his mother-tongue. But for the vttering fweetly, and properly the conceits of the minde, which is the end of fpeech, that hath it equally with any other tongue in the world : and is particulerly happy, in compofitions of two or three words together, neere the Greeke, far beyond the Latine : which is one of the greateft beauties can be in a language.

Now, of verfifying there are two forts, the one Auncient, the other Moderne : the Auncient marked the quantitie of each filable, and according to that, framed his verfe : the Moderne, obferuing onely number, (with fome regarde of the accent,) the chiefe life of it, ftandeth in that lyke founding of the words, which wee call Ryme.   VVhether of thefe be the moft excellent, would beare many fpeeches.   The Auncient, (no doubt) more fit for Mufick, both words and tune obferuing quantity, and more fit liuely to expreffe diuers pafsions, by the low and lofty founde of the well-weyed filable   The latter likewife, with hys Ryme, ftriketh a certaine mufick to the eare : and in fine, fith it dooth delight, though by another way, it obtaines the fame purpofe : there beeing in eyther fweetnes, and wanting in neither maieftie.   Truely the Englifh, before any other vulgar language I know, is fit for both forts : for, for the Ancient, the Italian is fo full of Vowels, that it muft euer be cumbred with *Elifions*.   The Dutch, fo of the other fide with Confonants, that they cannot yeeld the fvveet flyding, fit for

a Verſe. The French, in his whole language, hath
not one word, that hath his accent in the laſt ſilable,
ſauing two, called *Antepenultima*, and little more hath
the Spaniſh: and therefore, very graceleſly may they vſe
Dactiles. The Engliſh is ſubiect to none of theſe defects.

Nowe, for the ryme, though wee doe not obſerue
quantity, yet wee obſerue the accent very preciſely:
which other languages, eyther cannot doe, or will not
doe ſo abſolutely. That *Cæſura*, or breathing place
in the middeſt of the verſe, neither Italian nor Spaniſh
haue, the French, and we, neuer almoſt fayle of.
Laſtly, euen the very ryme it ſelfe, the Italian cannot
put in the laſt ſilable, by the French named the Mas-
culine ryme, but ſtill in the next to the laſt, which the
French call the Female; or the next before that,
which the Italians terme *Sdrucciola.* The example of
the former, is *Buono, Suono,* of the *Sdrucciola, Femina,
Semina.* The French, of the other ſide, hath both the
Male, as *Bon, Son,* and the Female, as *Plaiſe, Taiſe.* But
the *Sdrucciola,* hee hath not: where the Engliſh hath all
three, as *Due, True, Father, Rather, Motion, Potion;* with
much more which might be ſayd, but that I finde already,
the triflingnes of this diſcourſe, is much too much en-
larged. So that ſith the euer-praiſe-worthy Poeſie, is full of
vertue-breeding delightfulnes, and voyde of no gyfte,
that ought to be in the noble name of learning: ſith
the blames laid againſt it, are either falſe, or feeble:
ſith the cauſe why it is not eſteemed in Englande, is
the fault of Poet-apes, not Poets: ſith laſtly, our
tongue is moſt fit to honor Poeſie, and to bee honored
by Poeſie, I coniure you all, that haue had the euill
lucke to reade this incke-waſting toy of mine, euen in
the name of the nyne Muſes, no more to ſcorne the
ſacred miſteries of Poeſie: no more to laugh at the
name of Poets, as though they were next inheritours
to Fooles: no more to ieſt at the reuerent title of a
Rymer: but to beleeue with *Ariſtotle,* that they were
the auncient Treaſurers, of the Græcians Diuinity.
To beleeue with *Bembus,* that they were firſt bringers

in of all ciuilitie. To beleeue with *Scaliger*, that no Philofophers precepts can fooner make you an honeſt man, then the reading of *Virgill.* To beleeue with *Clauſerus*, the Tranſlator of *Cornutus*, that it pleafed the heauenly Deitie, by *Heſiod* and *Homer*, vnder the vayle of fables, to giue vs all knowledge, Logick, Rethorick, Philofophy, naturall, and morall; and *Quid non?* To beleeue with me, that there are many miſteries contained in Poetrie, which of purpofe were written darkely, leaſt by prophane wits, it ſhould bee abufed. To beleeue with *Landin*, that they are fo beloued of the Gods, that whatfoeuer they write, proceeds of a diuine fury. Laſtly, to beleeue themſelues, when they tell you they will make you immortall, by their verſes.

Thus doing, your name ſhal floriſh in the Printers ſhoppes; thus doing, you ſhall bee of kinne to many a poeticall Preface; thus doing, you ſhall be moſt fayre, moſt ritch, moſt wife, moſt all, you ſhall dwell vpon Superlatiues. Thus dooing, though you be *Libertino patre natus*, you ſhall fuddenly grow *Hercules proles*:
Si quid mea carmina poſſunt.
Thus doing, your soule ſhal be placed with *Dantes Beatrix*, or *Virgils Anchiſes.* But if, (fie of fuch a but) you be borne fo neere the dull making *Cataphraȼ* of *Nilus*, that you cannot heare the Plannet-like Muſick of Poetrie, if you haue fo earth-creeping a mind, that it cannot lift it felfe vp, to looke to the ſky of Poetry: or rather, by a certaine ruſticall difdaine, will become fuch a Mome, as to be a *Momus* of Poetry: then, though I will not wiſh vnto you, the Aſſes eares of *Midas*, nor to bee driuen by a Poets verſes, (as *Bubonax* was) to hang himfelfe, nor to be rimed to death, as is fayd to be doone in Ireland: yet thus much curfe I muſt fend you, in the behalfe of all Poets, that while you liue, you liue in loue, and neuer get fauour, for lacking ſkill of a *Sonnet*: and when you die, your memory die from the earth, for want of an *Epitaph.*

FINIS.

www.ingramcontent.com/pod-product-compliance
Lightning Source LLC
Chambersburg PA
CBHW021530270326
41930CB00008B/1176